ISBN 978-0-266-20670-5
PIBN 10211546

ON

FEDERAL GOVERNMENTS,

PAST AND PRESENT.

BY

THE HON. THOS. D'ARCY McGEE, M.R.I.A.

.WITH AN APPENDIX, CONTAINING THE FEDERAL CONSTI-
TUTION OF THE NEW ZEALAND COLONIES.

"I would form an individual model, suited to the character, disposition, wants,
and circumstances of the country, and I would make all exertions, whether by
action or by writing, within the limits of the existing law, for ameliorating its
existing condition, and bringing it nearer to the model selected for imitation."—
SIR GEO. CORNEWALL LEWIS.—*A Dialogue on the best form of Government.*
page 117.

Montreal:
PUBLISHED BY DAWSON BROTHERS.
1865.
Price 25 Cents.

NOTES

ON

FEDERAL GOVERNMENTS,

PAST AND PRESENT.

BY

THE HON. THOS. D'ARCY McGEE, M.R.I.A.

WITH AN APPENDIX, CONTAINING THE FEDERAL CONSTI-
TUTION OF THE NEW ZEALAND COLONIES.

"I would form an individual model, suited to the character, disposition, wants,
and circumstances of the country, and I would make all exertions, whether by
action or by writing, within the limits of the existing law, for ameliorating its
existing condition, and bringing it nearer to the model selected for imitation."—
SIR GEO. CORNEWALL LEWIS.—*A Dialogue on the best form of Government.*
page 117.

Montreal:
PUBLISHED BY DAWSON BROTHERS.
1865.

JOHN LOVELL, PRINTER.

To His Excellency

The Right Hon. Charles Stanley Viscount Monck,

Governor-General of British North America, &c., &c.,

This Contribution to the discussion of the subject

Most interesting to these Provinces,

Is, by permission,

Respectfully Dedicated.

MONTREAL, Dec. 24th, 1864.

CONTENTS.

PAGE.

I.—On the Federal Government of the Greeks,   7

II.—The Italian Leagues of the Middle Ages.. 17

III.—The Swiss Confederation............... 21

IV.—The United Provinces of the Netherlands.. 26

V.—The German Confederation 30

VI.—The United States.................... 34

VII.—The Confederate States. 41

VIII.—The New Zealand Confederation 45

IX.—Conclusion 51

Appendix................................. 54

I.—ON THE FEDERAL GOVERNMENT OF THE GREEKS.

MR. GROTE concludes his admirable History of Greece with the exploits and death of Alexander (B.C. 323). It is certainly a striking and appropriate conclusion. In the twelve years' reign of the Macedonian conqueror, the Hellenic genius seemed to blaze up to its utmost height, to cast its far reflections over the whole earth, to waver, to subside, and almost to expire. For an epic close to an epic story, the career of that earlier " scourge of God," so splendid in his rise, so resistless in his prime, so lamentable in his death, could not have been equalled. But withdrawing our attention, even from such a personage as Alexander, and freeing ourselves, by an effort, from the fascinations of such a writer as Mr. Grote, we dare unite in opinion with those who hold, that the century after the great conqueror's death, is not the least glorious or instructive in Grecian history. This was the century when the famous Federations, or Leagues, of Ætolia and Achaia, with their lesser imitators, played so important a part in the affairs, not only of Greece proper, but of the whole Hellenic world. It was the century of the foundation of Greek dynasties at Alexandria and Antioch ; the century of the Antigonid kings in Macedon ; of Phokion and Demetrius at Athens ; of Aratos and Philopoimên among the Achaians ; and of Kleomines in Sparta. But the political characteristic which, of all others, commends it most to our attention, is the disposition to federalize, then first followed out, practically and perseveringly, by the Greeks of the fatherland.

No trait of public character was more invariable in the

earlier and better known ages of Greece, than the jealousy
with which each community guarded its own autonomy. The
hundred and fifty constitutions which Aristotle collected, in
the age of Alexander, represented, of course, as many distinct
governments or states. The majority of these "states"
were mere city commonwealths, bounded by their walls and
their galleys, standing for centuries almost within sight of
each other, speaking the same speech, and worshipping the
same gods ; but without a particle of the insatiate Roman
thirst for centralization. They had, indeed, in the Panhellenic
festivals a substitute, which seems to have served them, at
one time, in the stead of national unity. To these great
periodical gatherings on the banks of the Alpheus and the
shores of the Isthmus, the Greeks of Marseilles, of Emporia,
of Syracuse, of Kyrêne, of Sinope, and of Bosporus, and
Borysthenes, were free to come. Champions entering for the
games, were considered, like ambassadors, sacred in their
persons ; and the farther removed, in point of residence, the
victor might be, the greater, in those few short days of glorious confraternity, was accounted the lustre thrown upon
the ancestral soil by his achievements.

But the games and rites once over, the self-willed communities fell back upon their jealous autonomy ; and all
the fine songs of fraternity chaunted in chorus by colonists
and old-countrymen, were exchanged for the keenest and
most grasping selfishness. This, perhaps, was the main secret
of Grecian decay. Intellectually the first of races, they had
yet one cardinal defect of character—they lacked the power
of sustained political combination. In their happier times
they did not so much need or miss this essential quality in a
truly great people ; but when, within two lives, Macedon
rose to the rank of the first military empire of the earth,—
when they found this fiercer Persia established on their own
frontier as a perpetual menace,—then the last statesmen of
Greece, worthy of the name, saw the necessity of bringing

about a union of the autonomous governments, for their mutual safety and defence.

Of these unions, the two most celebrated were, the Ætolian League and the Achaian; the former dating from long before Alexander, and continuing till its submission to Rome (about 180 B.C.); the latter first rising into notice about B.C. 280, and continuing till its turn came to submit to Rome, B.C. 145. We have thus a century and a half of Achaian Federalism; and a much longer period (but with far fewer lights to guide us through it) of Ætolian Federalism. The scholars of Germany have labored with their proverbial industry to illustrate this, as well as every other phase of Grecian public life; and among ourselves, Bishop Thirlwall, in his last volume, and Mr. Freeman,* in his first, have collected together almost all that is possible to be known upon the subject.

At the period of its greatest extent, the Ætolian Confederacy included the whole of Northern Greece, bordering on Thessaly and Epirus, a part of Central Greece (including at one time Delphi), and the islands of Têos and Kios, in the Ægean Sea. The Ætolians proper were mountain tribes, of admitted Hellenic stock, but of very inferior Hellenic culture. They had, however, in a higher degree than others of the Greeks, the constitutional virtues of obedience and subordination; and their league was, consequently, the longest-lived and the most highly centralized known to that people. It was a league of districts rather than of cities; and in the diversity of its elements, as well as its geographical position, bore some general resemblance to Switzerland—with her city-cantons and forest-cantons. The Constitution was, in the Greek sense, democratic—that is to say, in our modern sense, aristocratic. The general assembly, which met for "despatch of business," usually at the autumnal equinox, at whatever place it might

---

* History of Federal Governments. London and Cambridge: McMillan. & Co. 1863. Vol. I. *Greek Federations.*

be summoned, was primary; that is, every free citizen had the right to be present, to speak, and to vote. Practically, only the chieftains of the hill-tribes, and the wealthier inhabitants of the more settled districts attended. The executive power was constituted of the apokletoi, or senate, a sort of committee of the assembly, numbering at one time as high as thirty members; a commander-in-chief; a master of horse; and an official answering to our notions of a secretary of state. The commander-in-chief was also president of the general assembly; but he had neither voice nor vote in its deliberations. He could, however, summon special meetings; and he also seems to have presided in the highest court of justice. The magistracy, coinage, and taxation, beside the sovereign powers of peace and war, were all subject to the federal authority. As a general rule, the Ætolians are always spoken of by cotemporary writers as one people; and though their annals are not always free from reproach, it is certain that in resisting the Gaulish invasion of Greece (B.C. 279), and in the unhappy Lamian war (B.C. 322), they bore a most honorable part. On entering into alliance with the Romans, they made very favorable conditions; but their place in history knows them no more.

The Achaian League differed from the Ætolian in many important particulars. It was strictly a league of cities, of which modern research has enumerated not less than seventy. Of these about one-half joined the Union during the first forty years of its existence, while others continued to drop in down to the very hour of its dissolution. At its best, this government was supreme in Peloponnesus, garrisoning Akrôkôrinthos and Mantineia with Federal troops; and wielding the resources of such cities as Corinth, Sikyôn, Megalopolis, Megara, Argos, Pellênê, and others scarcely less populous. Aigion was at first the Federal capital; but Philopoimên, (B.C. 194) introduced the system of meeting in the principal cities by rotation,—a change which is thought by some historians to have hastened the downfall of the government it was intended to strengthen.

The Achaian Constitution consisted in the first place of a primary general assembly, convoked twice a year ; a committee of the assembly acting as a sort of senate ; a commander-in-chief, chosen annually ; with a council of ten. The commander-in-chief was also the leader, if not the president of the general assembly, and seems to have centred in his own person the highest civil as well as military powers. No citizen could fill this office two years in succession, as we learn from the life of the all-powerful Aratos, who was compelled to rest content with being in command every second year. As the sessions of the general assembly rarely exceeded three days in duration, the real power rested with the commander-in-chief, his council, and the senatorial committee or commission.

It is now more than eighty years ago since the two closest students of Federal principles that America has produced,* observed, " Could the interior structure and regular operation of the Achaian League be ascertained, it is probable that more light might be thrown by it on the science of Federal government, than by any of the like experiments with which we are acquainted." Recent researches, the results of which may be briefly stated, have gone a long way to supply this *desideratum*, as pointed out in the *Federalist*.

It seems certain the general government, under the Achaian Constitution, was sovereign ; that it sent and received ambassadors, enlisted and maintained troops, coined money, and performed other acts of sovereignty. As in all Greek communities—except the avowed monarchies—the final vote, on peace, or war, or foreign alliances, was submitted to the people—that is, to the general assembly. The assembly, though open to all freemen, was practically in the

---

* Madison and Hamilton.—*Federalist*, No. 18 (a joint composition).

hands of what a modern democrat would call the aristocracy —the best educated men, of wealth, leisure, and good family. The vote, however, was taken by cities, not by the poll, which would seem to imply some sort of delegation of authority to those who were to speak for all their fellow-citizens. Each city had but one vote—an arbitrary arrangement, irrespective of the wealth or power of the city, which must have been felt to be unjust by such communities as Corinth and Argos, when they were outvoted by Aigion, and towns of that size. The only Confederation of antiquity which seems to have graduated the votes of its members, with reference to their relative importance, was the Lykian League. But Lykia was a non-Hellenic State, and is not now under consideration.

From the extreme shortness of the popular session, as Mr. Freeman remarks, it is evident the initiation of almost *all* measures to be submitted to the assembly must have devolved on the government. At an extraordinary session, from the very nature of the emergency, this must have been more exclusively so. The council of ten—one from each of ten cities, afterwards enlarged—seems to have sat, in executive session, as is the case at Washington; but with some material points of difference. It often sat when the assembly did not; assisted in preparing measures for the assembly; and received and heard ambassadors, after the Roman manner. There does not appear to have been any system of Federal taxation established; but in its stead requisitions were made annually, for a certain contingent contribution, from the different cities. The commander-in-chief had authority to call out the whole military force of the Confederates; but there was in addition a standing Federal force, of whom a certain proportion were mercenary troops.

The lives of Aratos and Philopoimên, the greatest statesman and the greatest soldier of the Achaian Union, must be familiar to all readers of Polybius and Plutarch.

Aratos was born at Sikyon, on the bay of Corinth, B.C. 271. At the age of seven he, of all his family, escaped with life from a local tyrant who had usurped the city. Educated at Argos, the youthful exile, at the age of twenty, by a night surprise as daring as anything in history, delivered his native city from her tyrant, without the effusion of blood. In that hour he laid the foundations of a popularity which he never wholly lost; which placed him twelve or thirteen several times at the head of the Achaians, and gave him the first place among the Greeks of his day.

The policy of Aratos, during the nearly forty years of his domination, at first led him to lean on that one of Alexander's successors, established in Egypt, rather than on Macedon. He endeavored to use, and not without success, the Ptolemies against the Antigonids. Egypt was not too far for an ally, while Macedon was near enough for an enemy. The aid he chiefly derived from Alexandria was money; of which Ptolemy Philadelphos is said to have given him from time to time 170 talents. By him the Macedonian garrison was surprised and expelled from Akrôkôrinthos, the key of the Peloponnesus. By him Corinth, Megara, Megalopolis, Argos, and other great cities, were brought into the Union. The dream of his life was to have added Athens to the rest, either by persuasion or conquest; but the degenerate capital of Attica preferred its nominal autonomy and real dependence on Macedon, to the headship of the noblest native alliance ever formed in Greece. When Phokion was the first in authority, and the living Demetrius was worshipped as a god, no wonder Aratos failed in all his efforts. With the Spartan kings, the Bœotians, and the Ætolian league, he at first formed an alliance against Macedon, for what was called "the Demetrian war," one battle in which, at least, was fought as far northward as Thessaly. The shifting necessities of the allies, however, soon ranged them upon opposite sides. The Ætolians made peace with Macedon; while the Spartans who, under Agis, fought side by side with the Achaians, became, under Kleomines, the most formidable assailants of the united cities. In three campaigns (B.C. 226-224), the Spartans won three pitched battles over the Achaians, and otherwise broke their ascendancy in Southern Greece. Kleomines himself would willingly have joined the Union, but only on condition of making Sparta its capital, and himself its general. Rather than submit to this dictation, the Federal assembly agreed (B.C. 224) to invite the king of Macedon into Peloponnesus, as a protector ; a fatal alternative, which embittered the last years, if it did not literally occasion the death, of Aratos. At this period, the true policy of Greece, could her States and statesmen have seen it, as Isocrates had long before advocated, and Agelaos and other patriotic Greeks again contended, might have been a general Union, under the headship of Macedon. Macedon was the northern barrier of Greece, and the Romans were already established in Illyria. But instead of a closer Union, we find the Achaian League, engaged on one side, and the Ætolian League, on the other, in the suicidal " Social War." We need not be surprised, if in another generation Rome had swallowed up the Ætolians, and in yet another, the Achaians themselves.

After the death of Aratos (B.C. 213), the last stand was made for Federal Greece, by Philopoimên, of Megalopolis. The Romans call this illustrious man, " the last of the Greeks;" and Plutarch tells us, " Greece loved him exceedingly, as the child of her old age." He was, however, the very opposite of Aratos, a daring and capable soldier, rather than a profound statesman. His greatest political successes were, bringing Sparta into the league, and keeping the Union intact against the intrigues of the Romans. He was for the eighth time general, when, in the 70th year of his age (B.C. 183), he was captured by the Messenians, who had seceded from the Union, and died the death of Socrates and Demosthenes, taking poison in prison. " He left the

League,'" says Mr. Freeman, " if not what it once had been, yet as flourishing and as independent as any State could hope to be in those evil times. Achaia was still the first of existing republics, the compeer of any existing kingdom." For nearly forty years longer the league continued to exist, at least in name, till the final subjection of Southern Greece by the Consul Mummius (B.C. 147), who was honored by his countrymen therefor, with the surname of *Achaiacus*.

Of the other Federations of the Greeks, though far from being obscure in their time, we have too scanty records to enable us to give a detailed description.

NOTE ON THE LYKIAN LEAGUE.

The Lykian League—though not the work of an Hellenic people, exceeded anything known to the Greeks, in the completeness of its parts. The records of its origin are lost with the language of its citizens; but we have several Roman notices of it from B.C. 188, to its incorporation into the Empire, under Claudius, (A.D. 50.) In Strabo, the Geographer's time (A.D. 25), it consisted of three and twenty cities; which cities met in a common assembly, wherever they choose; the greater cities had three votes each; and the lesser, one. There seems to have been a senate as well as a general assembly. By these bodies the Lykiarch, or chief magistrate was chosen; the Federal judges, and other magistrates. Before its alliance with Rome, the Federal power concluded peace, or made war, contracted alliances, coined money, &c., &c. The outlines of this Constitution have excited the admiration of many high political authorities, considering the state of knowledge which prevailed in the ages when it was in being.

II.—The Italian Leagues of the Middle Ages.

To the beginning of the eleventh century, Muratori traces the rise of the greater part of the independent governments of Italy, and to the last half of the twelfth, their first attempts at Confederation.

The earliest of the Italian Leagues, like those of Greece, arose out of a great military necessity. Frederick Barbarossa having been crowned emperor, at Aix-la-Chapelle, in the year 1152, commenced at once that series of Italian aggressions which ceased only with his crusade and death—A.D. 1190. The city of Milan, as it was the chief object of his hostility, so it had the honor as well as the foresight to bring about the first Lombard League. In the tenth year of Frederick's reign, this great city, the churches excepted, was laid in ashes ; but from those ashes arose the first and most celebrated of the Italian Unions. Originally the league consisted of seventeen cities, and the Marquisate of Malaspina. In 1176, the army of the League won the glorious victory of Legnano ; and seven years later they obtained their own conditions of peace, by the treaty of Constance.*

The league of Lombardy, originally entered into for a period of twenty years, was, from time to time, prolonged or renewed, down to the beginning of the Fourteenth century, when the great family of the Visconti, overgrowing all other influences, changed the consular and elective government into a ducal and hereditary power. In the century and a half,

---

* For the rise of the Lombard League, see Sismondi, "Italian Republics," Vol. I. chap. X, and Vol. II, chap. I.

which thus elapsed, the Constitution of the league was rather military than political,—each city preserving its own consul or podesta, and secret or executive council. Though there was no permanent central authority, occasional congresses of the rulers of the several cities were held. Thus assembled they were called *Rectores Societatis Lombardiæ ;* but their functions seem to have been simply consultative, without legislative or executive powers *per se.* Each consul or podesta reported to his council or city; and the whole of the citizens, in primary assembly, had the final right to pronounce upon any fundamental change in the Constitution, and also, it appears, on all questions of alliance, peace, and war.

The main defects in the Lombard League, and that of the cities of Tuscany, formed after that model, were: 1. The temporary and precarious conditions of the Union; 2. Permitting each member of it to treat separately with foreign powers; 3. The jealousy of those in power, begetting, on their part, the necessity of placing themselves above the reach of their electors. In Florence, by one ordinance, thirty-seven noble families were declared forever incapable of holding office. In Milan and other cities the podesta was always a native of another state ; he could not marry within the limits of his government, nor could any of his relatives reside near him ; nor could he eat or drink in the house of any citizen. Sometimes this officer, who had a fixed annual salary, united the highest military and judicial authority, but more commonly his office was simply judicial. The law, of course, was the Roman law, of which, as well as of classical learning, Federal Italy was the great restorer.

The league of Tuscany was founded in imitation of that of Lombardy, with the addition of a strong ecclesiastical element, infused into it by its greatest promoter, Pope Innocent III. The chief civil authority was vested in three Priors, of whom the poet Dante, in the year 1300, was one. There was also a military chief,—the Gonfalionere,—who led the urban and rural militia in war.*　In the year 1421, this office was filled by Giovanni de Medici, a merchant and politician, who may be considered the founder of that cele-brated family which was destined to give Dukes to Tuscany, Queens to France, and Pontiffs to Rome.

The jealousy between the plebeian and patrician orders in the state, manifested itself by many other signs besides the personal restrictions imposed on the podestas of Lombardy. The Florentine Priors were elected only for a term of two months, during which time they were obliged to lodge and eat together, and not to absent themselves from the palace. The Tuscan trades were organized into guilds and close cor-porations, each with its own officers, arms, and standard. In the Lombard capital, the first political democratic clubs, *la Motta*, and *la Credenza*, exercised a powerful influence. But the patricians, in every instance, triumphed in the end. Nor was this revolution effected in all cases without the con-sent of the people.　Weary of the feuds, the proscriptions, and the instability of their defective and precarious leagues, they sanctioned the usurpations of able and energetic men, like the Visconti and the Medici, as an escape from anarchy.

Yet notwithstanding the very imperfect form of Federation by which the Tuscan and Lombard cities were governed during the whole of the thirteenth century, they prospered and were greatly distinguished under that *regime*.　A cotemporary writer reckons the population of Milan in 1288 at 200,000, while the province could bring into the field 8,000 cava-liers (*milites*), and 240,000 men capable of bearing arms. Among other elements of the city population, there are enu-merated 600 notaries, 200 physicians, eighty schoolmasters, and fifty transcribers of manuscripts.　On the discovery of

---

* In 1337, Florence (*qy.*, the Tuscan League ?) could bring 80,000 men into the field ; and the annual revenue was estimated at 300,000 florins. (Sismondi *passim*.)　In 1405, Florence acquired Pisa by purchase ; and in 1420, purchased the port we call Leghorn.

printing, both Milan and Florence became leading seats of the new art; but Venice, in her peaceful and prosperous isolation, soon surpassed, in the number and excellence of her printers, the distracted and degenerate relics of both Confederacies.

To Italy, in these ages, we owe the regular establishment of consuls and ambassadors ; the first attempts at a balance of power ; the revival of Roman law and classical studies ; the great Italian schools of art ; the inventions of book-keeping and banking ; and the discovery of America. It was the age also of the great masters of the Italian language, in prose and verse, from Dante to Machiavelli and Ariosto.

An attempt to establish a Federal government for all Italy, was made by the Roman tribune, Rienzi, during his first administration—A.D. 1347. " Could passion," says Gibbon, in describing this attempt, " have listened to reason ; could private interest have yielded to the public welfare, the supreme tribunal and Confederate union of the Italian republic might have healed their intestine discord, and closed the Alps against the Barbarians of the North. But the propitious season had elapsed; and if Venice, Florence, Sienna, Perugia, and many inferior cities offered their lives and fortunes to the *good estate*, the tyrants of Lombardy and Tuscany must despise or hate the plebeian author of a free Constitution."*

We have seen, in our own days, a project of Italian Confederation emanating from an immeasurably more influential author than Rienzi, and meeting with no better success.

---

* Decline and Fall, chap. LXX.

III.—THE SWISS CONFEDERATION.

AN old German rhyme says:

> " When the lowly wept, and tyrants stormed,
> The Swiss Confederacy was formed."

THE heroic story of William Tell—told as it is in such a scene—has been, no doubt, overlaid with fictitious details ; but the Confederation of thirty-one Swiss and Swabian cities in the year 1385, with the defeat and death of the Emperor Leopold, at Sempach, in the next year, are well established historical incidents. The independence thus asserted by the Swiss was jealously maintained, with or without the Swabian alliance, during a century of intermittent war. In the year 1474, Louis XI, of France, invaded the Confederacy unsuccessfully ; and in 1477, after the three great defeats of Granson, Morat, and Nancy, Charles the Bold of Burgundy, forfeited his life and possessions in a mad attempt to subjugate the same people. In 1498, the Emperor Maximilian made a last effort to bring Switzerland back to its old allegiance ; but after two campaigns, conducted by the mountaineers with their proverbial heroism, he was compelled to declare thirteen cantons free from the jurisdiction of the imperial chamber, and from all imperial contributions (A.D. 1499). The annals of Switzerland, subsequent to its struggles against Austria, France, and Burgundy, are chiefly interesting, as they illustrate the theory of the balance of power, and the workings of international law. In the treaty of Westphalia (A.D. 1648), the cantons were first formally recognized by the rest of Europe as a sovereign power. Theological disputes occupied the greater part of the seventeenth and eighteenth centuries, as was natural in the land of Zuinglius, Calvin, and Saint Francis de Sales—a land of earnest faith and stern sincerity. Three times the test of pure doctrine was submitted to the issue of arms, to the imminent danger of the liberties of both belligerents. At length an open separation took place: two diets were created; the Catholic cantons met at Lucerne, and the Protestant at Berne,—the former rejoicing in an alliance with France, and the latter with Holland. From thirteen, the number gradually increased to nineteen, by subdivision of old or acquisition of new districts,—when the perturbations of the French revolution shook them to the foundations. In 1798 they were metamorphosed into the Helvetic Republic; in 1803 they fell under the protectorate of Napoleon I; and in 1813 were consequently invaded by the Allies. By the Federal Act—signed at Zurich in August, 1815—an amended Constitution was established; and three months later the neutrality of Switzerland was recognized by the Allies, at Paris.

In 1830, and again in 1848, the cantons experienced the prevailing revolutionary paroxysm; but the democratic changes introduced, have been confined to the local Constitutions. Neufchatel has returned to its ancient relations to Prussia; and Berne has become the fixed Federal capital, instead of the former rotatory system, by which the Diet assembled in turn at Berne, Zurich, and Lucerne. The Federal Act of 1815 still remains in its integrity, the Constitution of all the united cantons.

This Constitution has evidently been borrowed in good part, from that of the United States of America, while retaining something of French revolutionary principles. The objects of the Union are declared to be the protection of the country against the foreigner; to secure tranquillity; protect the liberties of the Confederacy; and increase the general prosperity.

Art. 3 declares the cantons sovereign, except in such matters as are delegated to the Federal government;

Which, by Art. 8, is authorized to declare war, conclude peace, and enter into treaties of customs and commerce.

Art. 9 reserves to the cantons the right of making commercial treaties for themselves—provided they do not conflict with existing Federal treaties, or the rights of other cantons.

Art. 10 further explains this apparently inconsistent retention and delegation of powers.

Art. 18 declares all Swiss subject to military duty.

Art. 19. The contingent of each canton to the *élite* of the Confederation, is *three* men out of every *hundred* inhabitants. Subsequent articles contain the army regulations.

Art. 25 prescribes the extent to which Federal legislation may extend on customs. Imports in general may be taxed; raw material at the lowest, and luxuries at the highest, rate. A general power of taking exceptional measures in cases of emergency is granted.

Art. 26. Each canton shall receive of the product of the customs, at the rate of four *batz* per head for each inhabitant. Those cantons which have yielded their separate revenues, shall receive a further subsidy (if the above be insufficient), according to the product of certain specified years. The surplus over all, goes into the Federal treasury.

Art. 38 reserves the manufacture and sale of gunpowder exclusively to the Confederation.

Art. 39 defines the Federal revenues to be : 1, the interest of the war fund ; 2, frontier customs ; 3, postal revenue ; 4, product of powder sales ; 5, contributions from the cantons, specially levied.

Art. 42. The citizen of each canton is a citizen of all under the same conditions as native citizens.

Art. 68. The members of the Federal Council are paid from the *Federal* Exchequer.

By Art. 72, members of the *National* Council are paid by the cantons they represent.

These two Councils embody the whole legislative power.

The National Council—the popular body—is composed of one member for each 20,000 souls; meets annually; may be called specially by the Federal Council, (composed of one member from each canton), or on the requisition of five cantons. A majority of each Council must constitute a quorum: the Federal councillors are elected every third year; the National, every year.

The president and vice-president of the Confederation, (the latter of whom is, *ipso-facto*, president of the Federal Council), and the chancery, or secretariate, is filled by the election of the legislature. There is also a Federal tribunal (Arts. 100–101), to take cognizance of civil justice, saving special cantonal rights; of disputes arising between cantons; cases between any canton and the Confederation; and cases of the unnaturalized (*Heimathlose*).

Arts. 113 and 114 provide for amendments to the Constitution, which may originate with the Federal Council, or by 50,000 electors demanding the consideration of certain amendments. In all cases the amendments must be submitted to the *yea* or *nay* of the whole body of electors. For their adoption there must be not only a majority of electors, but a majority of cantons.*

The Diet directs the operations of the Federal army, appoints the commanding officers, sends and receives ambassadors.

This Constitution, which has withstood two European revolutions, besides its own internal trials, has lasted now, with some slight amendments, for fifty years. Of course, much must be allowed for the peculiar position and circumstances of Switzerland. But it ought not to be forgotten that the most various population in the world is embraced under this system. Of the whole two millions and a half, a million and

---

* Encyclopédie Théologique.—Dict. des Sciences, Pol. et Sociales, Vol. III, Art. *Switzerland*. Paris, 1855.

two-thirds speak German ; half a million French ; and the remainder Italian, and other tongues. The Alpine population is chiefly Catholic ; the city cantons chiefly Protestant. Differences of interest and locality ; differences of race and creed ; differences of speech and manners,—all are found in Switzerland,—yet all are free, and when unaggressive, each on the other, all are secure, respected, and prosperous, in their freedom.

IV.—THE UNITED PROVINCES OF THE NETHERLANDS.

———

THE " Seven United Provinces," or the "United States of the Netherlands," as they were irrespectively called, exhibit a very peculiar and instructive form of Confederation. In a territory of about 220 miles long by 140 wide,—a great portion of which had been reclaimed from the sea,—there flourished under the Emperor Charles V., seventeen populous communities, known to the rest of the world as duchies, counties and lordships, each with its own lord, its own assembly, its courts, militia, and taxation. At a general assembly of these communities convened at Brussels, in the year 1555, Charles V. solemnly resigned all his crowns and cares, and introduced to his subjects his son and successor, Phillip II.

The insurrection of the Netherlands against Phillip II. is one of the best known episodes in modern history. In the eleventh year of that Prince (A.D. 1566) the patriot party formed at a dinner table, in Brussels, the brotherhood of the *Gueux*, out of which sprung the insurrection. But the movement proceeded with true Dutch deliberation. It was not till 1580, that the States-general formally declared their independence of Spain, under a French protectorate ; nor till the treaty of Munster (A.D. 1648), that Spain formally renounced her ancient pretensions, and acknowledged the sovereignty of the Dutch Republic. By the general Treaty of Westphalia, the United Provinces entered formally, the same year, into the family of European nations.

The new Dutch Constitution was curiously complicated. Each Province retained its local control, not only over its own trade and taxation, but its sovereign right to treat with foreign States, at least, as to matters of commercial interest.

Within each Province were a number of co-equal self-governed cities, as jealous of their municipal independence as if they had been Greeks or Italians. From these Provinces and cities, deputies to the number of about fifty were sent to form the States-general at Amsterdam,—some elected for one year, some for three, some for six, some during pleasure, and some for life. The States-general were presided over by the Stadtholder, an office which became hereditary, but not without a long and bloody struggle, in the illustrious family of the Princes of Orange (A.D. 1629). The stadtholder not only was the president, so to speak, of the whole Union, but also of each Province, when he chose to discharge that function; he was also captain-general and admiral-general; sent and received ambassadors; exercised the prerogative of mercy; and enjoyed, before the French revolution, besides his vast patrimonial estates, a public provision of 300,000 florins per annum.

It was not without resistance that the oligarchies of the several Provinces, saw these monarchical prerogatives accumulate upon the House of Orange. The first resistance to such encroachments had been made by Barneveldt, Grotius, and the DeWitts; but Grotius died in exile, and the others were put to death. The name of DeWitt recalls the recollection of that anomalous official position—the Grand Pensionate of Holland.

The Province of Holland, from its greater maritime wealth and population, always exercised a disproportionate influence in the Confederacy. Its contribution to the Federal treasury was set down, by Sir William Temple, at fifty-eight per cent. of the whole. (Indeed, the *pro rata* contributions of the Provinces were little more than a constitutional fiction, and some of them have, in extreme cases, been collected only at the point of " the bayonet.") The chief civil officer in Holland was the Grand Pensionary. He was elected for a term of five years, and was paid a very moderate annual salary for his services.

He was enjoined to use all his efforts in preserving the liberties of Holland, yet to be strictly neutral in its internal disputes ; to watch over and report upon the finances of the Province, without the power to direct or diminish expenditure ; to hold correspondence with the ambassadors and allies of the Provinces abroad,—but he was to communicate no secret of state, except under authority of a resolution of the States-general! He was, in short, a very much hampered sort of secretary of state and the treasury, independent of the stadtholder, but absolutely at the mercy of the legislature. No wonder that even the genius and energy of a DeWitt should give way, under so responsible and so invidious an office !

The writers of the *Federalist* pointed the moral of this creation of inconsistent powers, eighty years ago, when they said, " a weak Constitution must necessarily terminate in dissolution, for want of proper powers, or from the usurpation of powers requisite for the public safety."* Some of these writers lived to see the anarchical system they so keenly dissected, overthrown by Bonaparte, and a kingdom of Holland established by the decree of Europe, in the Treaty of Vienna (A.D. 1815). Yet, with all its faults, it must be said the freedom of the United Provinces was alike favorable to their prosperity and celebrity. In the first century of their independence, the Dutch established themselves in the East Indies and America; they perfected the system of commercial exchanges, loans and annuities, which has ever since characterized European transactions ; they created a new school of art, to which we owe Rubens, Vandyke, and Teniers ; their

---

* "The true patriots" [of the Netherlands] have long bewailed the fatal operation of these vices [of their Constitution], and have made no less than four regular experiments by *extraordinary assemblies*, convened for the special purpose to apply a remedy. As many times has their laudable zeal found it impossible to unite the public Councils in reforming the known, the acknowledged, the fatal evils of the existing Constitution."—*Federalist*, No. XX.

scholarship was illustrated by Strada and Grotius : international law may be said to have risen full-armed from among them. Could they have united reverence for authority with the passion for freedom; could they have carried their intense love of order in private life, into their public business, the United Provinces, in all human probability, might still be counted among the foremost governments of the European continent.

V.—THE GERMAN CONFEDERATION.

BEFORE passing from Europe to the New World, the German Confederation remains to be mentioned.

The ancient empire, known to history for a thousand years as the Holy Roman-Germanic Empire, ceased to exist in 1806. On the 1st of August, Napoleon declared that he no longer recognized a German Empire ; on the 6th of the same month, Francis II. abdicated the Imperial Crown, and absolved his electors from their allegiance. Francis assumed the title of Emperor of Austria ; Bavaria, Wurtemberg and Holland were erected into kingdoms ; seventeen* Princes of Western Germany formed themselves by Napoleon's direction into *the Confederation of the Rhine*, while Prussia was invited to place herself at the head of a similar Confederation of Northern Germany. The successor of the great Frederick, who chose rather to try conclusions on the field of battle, was beaten to the earth, in a single campaign.

The Confederation of the Rhine was one of those governments which, according to the present Emperor of the French, his uncle determined to establish *ad interim*, while Europe was being prepared for his permanent system.† Foreign in its origin and its dependence ; living as it were by the breath of the conqueror who had humbled Austria and Prussia, and

---

* The Kings of Bavaria and Wurtemburg, the Grand Dukes of Frankfort, Wurzburg, Baden, Darmstadt, and Berg ; and the Princes of Nassau (two), Hohenzollern (two), Salm (two), and those of Aremberg Isenberg, Lichstenstein, and Leyden.

† *Considerations sur la Suisse;* an early pamphlet of Napoleon III.

abolished the ancient empire, it could hardly expect to become an object of respect to the German people. The Constitution was copied from the Helvetic model; the Federal Diet was to sit at Frankfort, under a Prince-Primate, nominated by Napoleon; while France was to retain control in all foreign affairs. Founded in an unpatriotic and un-German spirit, it fell without regret, after an inglorious seven years existence.

The idea of Confederation had, however, recommended itself to Germany, and found favor with the Allies congregated at Paris. Instead of attempting to restore the empire, a new species of union was devised and proclaimed, on the 8th June, 1815,—ten days before the final overthrow of Napoleon at Waterloo. This Constitution also owed its origin to foreign influence; contained in itself many fatal defects; and has been a fruitful source of agitation, ever since its adoption. In 1820, by the *Acte Finale* adopted at Vienna, several amendments were introduced; in 1832, the military organization of the Confederation was fixed by an organic law; but while the Diet has its own ways and means, the well known Zollverein, or Customs union, has never been adopted into the Federal system, and exists only by special compact, among individual States. Commercial intercourse, therefore, is not among the subjects with which the Diet has has to deal.

The free city of Frankfort-on-the-Maine is the seat of the Federal authority. The Diet sits in a two-fold capacity. In its first, or strictly federative capacity, no State casts more than one vote, while several small States unitedly cast one: thus from Austria to Saxony downward each has a single vote, while seven small duchies, and the four remaining "free cities," jointly, cast one. Austria presides over the Diet, by the 124th article of the Constitution as settled at Vienna, in 1815.

Whenever fundamental laws, or organic arrangements are to

be altered, or amended, the States of the first class cast four votes each ; of the second, three ; of the third, two ; and the fourth, one. Thus, in its federative capacity the whole vote of the Diet is seventeen; while in its popular capacity, it is seventy.

The attempt made in 1848, to revolutionize the League, and substitute in its stead a government proper, or more perfect Federation, having failed, the Constitution of 1815, with its amendments, still remains in force.

By Art. 11 the Confederation binds itself to defend the whole of Germany ; when it declares war, no State can enter into separate engagements with the enemy ; no State can enter into any alliance directed against the security of the Confederacy ; each State in its controversies with another binds itself to submit the same to a commission of the Diet in the first instance, and in the last to a Federal Tribunal, constituted for this purpose, from which there is no appeal.

By Art. 35 it is declared that the Confederation has the right to make war, conclude peace, and contract alliances, under the Federal Act.

By Art. 127 the right to send and receive ambassadors* is also asserted.

Arts. 36 to 49 detail the functions of the Diet, under the general provisions of Art. 35.

From a careful analysis of the Constitution, Dr. Phillimore educes the four following propositions :

First. That the Germanic Confederation maintains with those who are members of that league relations of a special international character resting entirely upon the Federal Act of 1815, and further explained by that of 1820, as their sole foundation; but that all the members of this league are governed in their relations with other independent States by the general international law.

Secondly. That the mutual rights and duties of the members of this Confederation are wholly distinct from those which exist between them and other States, not members of the Confederation.

Thirdly. That the operation of the duties and rights growing out of

* Phillimore's International Law, Vol. I, page 129.

the Constitution of the Confederation, is not only exclusively confined to the independent sovereigns who are members of it, but also to the territories which belong to them, by virtue of which they were originally incorporated into the Germanic Empire.

Fourthly. That the admission of new States, *not being German*, into the Confederation, or the admission of States *not sovereignties*, would conflict with the principle and the objects of the Confederation.

Notwithstanding the inherent weakness of the Federal League in Germany, it has certainly preserved the internal peace of the States that are parties to it, for half a century. It is to be hoped, that we shall never again see one German power straining every nerve, as in the Seven Years' War, in an unnatural attempt to dismember and destroy another.

VI.—THE UNITED STATES.

THE Constitution of the United States was a compromise between state jealousy and the strong sentiment of self-preservation; between the science and scholarship of such men as the authors of the *Federalist*, and the wild theories of the demagogues of the day. It betrays, therefore, very naturally, both in its strength and its weakness, in its provisions and omissions, the unmistakeable marks of this twofold parentage.

The revolutionary war had closed successfully for the original thirteen United States, with. the campaign of 1780. An armistice shortly followed; and a definite treaty of peace, between Great Britain and the United States, acknowledging the independence of the United States, was signed at Paris on the 3rd of September, 1783. While these negotiations were still pending, General Washington had addressed a circular letter to the governors of each of the States in favor of a more perfect union, and Alexander Hamilton, in his series of papers called *The Continentalist*, published at New York, and other writers, *pro* and *con*, opened up the whole subject of the relative powers of the state and general governments.

From the Declaration of Independence (1776) to the adoption of the Constitution (1789), the thirteen colonies existed under " Articles of Confederation," which articles, as compared with the more definite and authoritative system that followed, might be fairly taken to illustrate the *Federalists'* distinction between a " perfect " and " imperfect " Federation. Under the articles, Congress consisted of a single chamber, made up of delegates, annually appointed by the State legislatures, none of whom could, however, sit more than three years out of six. Each State maintained its own delegation, and each had one vote in Congress. The right was reserved to the States, with the concurrence of Congress, of raising troops, equipping armed vessels, imposing customs duties, making Indian wars, and entering into certain alliances. All warlike expenditure was to be repaid to each State in proportion to the valuation of its real property; but the collection of taxes to meet these payments was subject to the authority and direction of the local legislatures. Congress reserved to itself a general treaty-making power; the right of arbitrating between the States by Congressional commissioners; to coin money; to make loans on the general credit; to raise forces by land and sea; and to appoint a commander-in-chief, *provided*, in the two last cases, that *nine* out of the *thirteen* States concurred.

As to the executive power, it was exercised—so far as it existed at all—by a president of Congress, who could serve only one year in three; and by a " Committee of States," composed of one delegate from each State, whose functions were in some sort senatorial, except that they continued in existence during the recesses of Congress. The general body might be convoked anywhere within the Union, and no adjournment could be for a longer period than six months.*

After several years' trial of this sort of " league," (as it was correctly called in the Articles themselves,) the leading and best minds among the Americans became convinced that the then Constitution was wholly inadequate to the ends of government. Among those who were most instrumental in converting the Confederacy into a National Government, were, Washington, Hamilton, Madison, Jay, Adams, Wilson, King, Franklin, the Morrisses, Pinckneys, Carrolls, Roger

---

* By Art. XI. provision was made for the admission of Canada into the Union, on "joining in the measures of the United States," but no other colony could be admitted unless by the vote of *nine* States.

Sherman of Connecticut, and John Rutledge of South Caro-lina. Most of these eminent men were members of the last convention by which the Constitution was adopted. But their services were not confined to the convention chamber. By private correspondence, by published essays, by learned speeches, by delegations to and fro, they succeeded, after nearly ten years' advocacy, in securing for their new *Magna Charta* the approval of *eleven* out of· the thirteen States—some of them, it must be added, by very bare majorities.

The Constitution of the United States is an instrument so easily accessible to Canadians, as to render any analysis of its provisions unnecessary. It may, however, be proper to point out briefly wherein it differed from the former articles of Confederation. The new instrument divided the legislature into two chambers; the popular chamber representing num-bers, the senate representing co-equal States: money bills to originate only in the former; impeachments to originate in the House of Representatives, and be tried by the senate. The vice-president of the United States to possess the same qualification for election as the president; to preside over the senate; with right of succession to the presidency. The president to be commander-in-chief, with the power of a veto over all congressional legislation, unless re-enacted by a two-thirds vote of both houses. The subjects of congressional legislation are enumerated as follows, in Art. 1:

Sec. VIII.—The Congress shall have power—

1. To lay and collect taxes, duties, imposts, and excises; to pay the debts and provide for the common defence and general welfare of the United States; but all duties, imposts, and excises shall be uniform throughout the United States:

2. To borrow money on the credit of the United States:

3. To regulate commerce with foreign nations, and among the several States, and with the Indian tribes:

4. To establish a uniform rule of naturalization, and uniform laws on the subject of bankruptcies, throughout the United States:

5. To coin money, regulate the value thereof, and of foreign coin, and fix the standard of weights and measures:

6. To provide for the punishment of counterfeiting the securities and current coin of the United States :

7. To establish post-offices and post-roads :

8. To promote the progress of science and useful arts, by securing, for limited times, to authors and inventors, the exclusive right to their respective writings and discoveries :

9. To constitute tribunals inferior to the supreme court:

10. To define and punish piracies and felonies committed on the high seas, and offences against the law of nations :

11. To declare war, grant letters of marque and reprisal, and make rules concerning captures on land and water :

12. To raise and support armies; but no appropriation of money to that use shall be for a longer term than two years :

13. To provide and maintain a navy :

14. To make rules for the government and regulation of the land and naval forces.

15. To provide for calling forth the militia to execute the laws of the Union, suppress insurrections, and repel invasions :

16. To provide for organizing, arming and disciplining the militia, and for governing such parts of them as may be employed in the service of the United States, reserving to the states respectively the appointment of the officers, and the authority of training the militia, according to the discipline prescribed by Congress :

17. To exercise exclusive legislation, in all cases whatsoever, over such district (not exceeding ten miles square) as may, by cession of particular states, and the acceptance of Congress, become the seat of government of the United States, and to exercise like authority over all places purchased by the consent of the legislature of the state in which the same shall be, for the erection of forts, magazines, arsenals, dockyards, and other needful building : and,

18. To make all laws which shall be necessary and proper for carrying into execution the foregoing powers, and all other powers vested by this Constitution in the government of the United States, or in any department or officer thereof.

While the limits of the State governments are thus negatively defined:

Sec. IX.—1. The migration or importation of such persons as any of the states, now existing, shall think proper to admit, shall not be prohibited by the Congress prior to the year one thousand eight hundred and eight : but a tax or duty may be imposed on such importation, not exceeding ten dollars for each person.

2. The privilege of the writ of habeas corpus shall not be suspended

unless when, in cases of rebellion or invasion, the public safety may require it.

3. No bill of attainder, or ex post facto law, shall be passed.

4. No capitation or other direct tax shall be laid, unless in proportion to the census or enumeration herein before directed to be taken.

5. No tax or duty shall be laid on articles exported from any state. No preference shall be given, by any regulation of commerce or revenue, to the ports of one state over those of another; nor shall vessels bound to or from one state be obliged to enter, clear, or pay duties in another.

6. No money shall be drawn from the treasury, but in consequence of appropriations made by law; and a regular statement and account of the receipts and expenditures of all public money shall be published from time to time.

7. No title of nobility shall be granted by the United States; and no person holding any office of profit or trust under them, shall, without the consent of the Congress, accept of any present, emolument, office or title of any kind whatever, from any king, prince or foreign state.

SEC. X.—1. No state shall enter into any treaty, alliance, or confederation; grant letters of marque and reprisal; coin money; emit bills of credit; make anything but gold and silver coin a tender in payment of debts; pass any bill of attainder, ex post facto law, or law impairing the obligation of contracts; or grant any title of nobility.

2. No state shall, without the consent of Congress, lay any imposts or duties on imports or exports, except what may be absolutely necessary for executing its inspection laws; and the net produce of all duties and imposts laid by any state on imports or exports, shall be for the use of the treasury of the United States; and all such laws shall be subject to the revision and control of the Congress. No state shall, without the consent of Congress, lay any duty on tonnage, keep troops or ships of war in time of peace, enter into any agreement or compact with another state or with a foreign power, or engage in war, unless actually invaded, or in such imminent danger as will not admit of delay.

Art. 2 defines the nature, tenure, and responsibilities of the presidential office; Art. 3, of the Federal judiciary; Art. 4 treats of inter-state relations; Art. 5, of the power and mode of amending the Constitution; Art. 6, of the public debt, public obligations of each State, and qualifications for office; Art. 7, of the ratification and establishment of this Constitution. Ten amendments, in the nature of a " Bill of Rights," were proposed during the first session of the first Congress held under President Washington, and ratified in

December, 1791; one other amendment was proposed and adopted in 1798; and yet another in 1804. These *twelve* amendments, with the original articles, *seven* in number, form the fundamental law of the United States.

Before, during, after, and ever since the adoption of this Constitution of 1789, the great American controversy has been between State rights and Federal rights. The best minds of the first and second generations of that people have fully debated it; and the third generation have now sought to solve it by the arbitrament of the sword. Mr. Hamilton declares, in the last number of the *Federalist*, as of his own knowledge, that " powerful individuals," in New York and other States, were " *enemies* to a general national government, in every possible shape." Of this number, in Hamilton's sense, Jefferson might perhaps be counted ;* Patrick Henry, certainly; and there were others of hardly less mark. In the succeeding age, Mr. Calhoun and his school maintained the doctrine of " state rights," or rather state sovereignty, against Mr. Webster and his followers. On both sides the argument was marked by extraordinary ability. The true doctrine is not, unfortunately, on the face of the Constitution itself, by any means so clear, as to allow but one line of interpretation. Indeed, even Mr. Madison, who has been rather unmeasuredly called " the Father of the Constitution," is far from consistent with himself, in the various glosses he has given on this vital point of his own workmanship. We say, the true doctrine as to where the sovereignty resides in the American system is unfortunately by no means clear on the face of the Federal Act;—for what can be more unfortunate for a free people, than to be destitute of the essentials of stability and order in their government? What can be more fatal to the existence of a just and strong State, than an unsettled radical

---

* *Federalist*, No. 49.

question of right or wrong, as to which is the depository of sovereign power—the States or the Union? What verdict could be more crushing to any Constitution, than that half a century after its establishment, the foremost men, born and bred under its provisions, should be unable to agree as to whether it was the mere agent of the several States, or " a government proper?"

Still it would be most unfair to overlook the wonderful progress made by all the States, under this Union. The vast natural resources of the whole country had been explored and developed ; the complete freedom of inter-State trade had diffused wealth and activity to the farthest frontiers ; plenty and enjoyment had, for nearly a century, been the common inheritance of the whole people. Not much as yet had been done for the Fine Arts, but nowhere in the world, had the useful and practical been more successfully studied and improved. A new literature, too, had begun to manifest itself,—enriching and honoring the English language. In the midst of all these fruits and blossoms of peaceful progress, the original cause of controversy implanted in the Constitution, suddenly burst forth in an armed struggle between a portion of the States and the Federal power, the results of which are as yet hidden from our vision. One lesson, however, has been already taught to every just-minded observer of the still waging war, namely, that those who formerly held the Constitution of 1789 to be *perfect*, were not farther from the truth, than those who have since spoken of it as a complete *failure*.

VII.—The Confederate States.

———

The great State-rights controversy, which had been waged so fiercely over the very cradle of the United States Constitution—which had broken out so bitterly at every subsequent provocation—in 1812, 1817, 1821, 1833, 1850, and 1856,* —grew at length, in 1860, so incurably aggravated, that no further compromise could possibly be accepted. The election of Mr. Lincoln, on the basis of the Chicago Convention, led to an event which had been often foreseen and foretold—the forcible secession of the slaveholding States from the Union. The election was held in November; and on the 20th of December, 1860, South Carolina promulgated her ordinance of secession; in January, Mississippi, Florida, Alabama and Georgia followed; Texas joined the seceders in February, Virginia in April, Arkansas and North Carolina in May, and Tennessee in June. Delegates from all these States, with the addition of Kentucky, attended at the first regular Congress of the Confederate States, at Richmond, on the 12th of January, 1863. The total population thus represented, was within a fraction of eleven millions and a half; of which about 3,650,000 were slaves, and 150,000 free negroes.

The Constitution of the Confederacy, adopted at Montgomery, Alabama, on the 4th of February, 1861, one month previous to the inauguration of President Lincoln, was, in

———

* The first date represents the assertion of the principle by the New England States, against President Madison; the two following, what may be called the first and second Missouri Controversies; the others successively, the South Carolina "nullification" movement, the Texas annexation agitation, the Kansas-Nebraska Controversy, and the first election of President Lincoln.

many essential respects, a transcript of that of the United States. There were the same provisions as to the Constitution of the two Houses of Congress; the qualification of senators and representatives; the election and powers of the president and vice-president; the power of impeachment; the Habeas Corpus; religious liberty; the origination of money bills; and a Supreme Court. The principal departures from the original of 1789, in the new instrument were: 1. That the presidential term should continue for *six* instead of *four* years; while a second election is prohibited. 2. That the chief officer of each executive department may have a seat on the floor of either House, with right of speaking, but not of voting. 3. The "institution of negro slavery" as it exists, is recognized, with the right of extension into any future territory colonized from the Confederate States.

In the first of these Constitutional details, we see an effort made by the Southern statesmen to remedy that which from seventy years' experience, they believed to be a serious defect in the original they followed, the shortness of the presidential term, and the temptation presented by the re-eligibility of the incumbent, to convert his first term into a means of securing a second. In this respect, the Southerners boldly overcame that jealousy of power, which might have been expected from Seceders, and which, it is not difficult to foresee, must be the rock-ahead of their system. In the second provision, they advanced half way towards the British doctrine of ministerial accountability to the legislature; but there they halted. To give their ministers a seat merely in Congress, without a vote, seems neither to attain the object of the United States system, of holding the president accountable, even to impeachment, for his Cabinet; still less does it attain the object of the British, which, by holding the head of the State inviolable, yet maintains that he shall act only on advice, and thus makes responsible the advisers. But bred and practised as the Southern leaders mostly were in " democratic" theories of government, they deserve credit rather for attempting so much in the direction of permanency, than for not attempting more.

The distinguishing feature above all others of this Southern Constitution is, that it provides for a servile, or enslaved class, as a permanent basis of power. Saying nothing in this place of the morality or immorality of such a doctrine, it is to be remarked, that it is boldly, defiantly at war, with all the received opinions of Christendom. It is especially at war with the political dogmas which have gradually extended themselves over these new continents, North and South. For a new State to spring into existence, as it were, in a single night, with such a challenge to the whole civilized world, to establish as right and laudable what all others believe to be absolutely wrong, or at most tolerable, if temporary, was to burthen the new State with a weight of controversy, sufficient, in time, to depress all its energies and balance all its achievements. Apart altogether from the ethics of the question, I cannot but think it was a fatal error, politically, for the Montgomery Convention, (while rightly rejecting the proposition to reopen the African slave trade), that it did not also leave the whole subject of domestic slavery, an " open question."

NOTE.—*On the South American Confederacies.*

The Argentine Confederacy, as last remodelled in 1862, consists of *fourteen* Provinces, with local administrations for local purposes, and a Federal government ruling from Buenos-Ayres, over all. The president and vice-president are elected for six years; but I have not been able to obtain definite information, as to the other provisions of the new Constitution.

Brazil may be called a Monarchical Confederation of *twenty* Provinces. In 1815 Brazil was declared a kingdom, united with Portugal; in 1821 it was proclaimed independent, and an empire; in 1823 the present Federal Constitution was established. Both Houses of the general Congress are elective,—but neither by a direct popular vote. For the Senate, the electoral districts nominate three candidates, of whom the sovereign selects one; for the House of Congress, each two hundred electors choose a delegate, and the majority of delegates in a district, choose a deputy. The ministers of the sovereign are responsible, as in England, to the legislature and the country, for all official acts and advice given. The sovereign is inviolable. Titles of honor are conferred for life *only;* though they may be continued in the same family, for honorable cause, at the option of the emperor.

Brazil, it may be observed, is the only South American government which can boast half a century of immunity from anarchy and invasion. The other ephemeral Confederacies of that portion of the continent present few facts of sufficient interest to be repeated here.

VIII.—The New Zealand Confederation.

The latest application of Federal principles to the government of a new community (if we except the case of the Confederate States), is that of New Zealand, whose constitutional charter dates only from the 30th June, 1852.*

The European settlements in New Zealand are scattered in groups over two great and several small islands, hundreds of miles apart. Of these groups, nine Provinces have been formed, with a local elective superintendent and Council for each Province, and a general or Federal government over all ; with two chambers, a responsible Ministry, consisting of a colonial treasurer, colonial secretary, minister for native affairs, attorney-general, and a governor-general. The whole population in 1862, was estimated at 102,000 ; the revenue of the Union in 1860, at $2,320,690.

The able men, upon whose advice the New Zealand Constitution was mainly framed, were anxious above all things, to suit its provisions to the communities by whom they were to be carried into effect. They, therefore, localized administration to such extent, as the distance, state of intercourse, and local necessities required ; but they retained for the General government very large powers. The Upper House, consisting of twenty-four life members, and the Lower of fifty-three elective members, are alone competent to legislate on the following subjects of the first importance.

1. The Imposition or Regulation of Duties of Customs to be imposed on the Importation or Exportation of any Goods at any Port or Place in the Province :

* 15 and 16 Vic., cap. 72. As the only *British* precedent for a Federal Union, this Act is given in full, in an Appendix.

2. The Establishment or Abolition of any Court of Judicature of Civil or Criminal Jurisdiction, except Courts for trying and punishing such Offences as by the Law of *New Zealand* are or may be made punishable in a summary Way, or altering the Constitution, Jurisdiction, or Practice of any such Court, except as aforesaid

3. Regulating any of the current Coin, or the Issue of any Bills, Notes, or other Paper Currency :

4. Regulating the Weights and Measures to be used in the Province or in any Part thereof :

5. Regulating the Post Offices and the Carriage of Letters within the Province :

6. Establishing, altering, or repealing Laws relating to Bankruptcy or Insolvency :

7. The Erection and Maintenance of Beacons and Lighthouses on the Coast :

8. The Imposition of any Dues or other Charges on Shipping at any Port or Harbour in the Province :

9. Regulating Marriages :

10. Affecting Lands of the Crown, or Lands to which the Title of the aboriginal native Owners has never been extinguished :

11. Inflicting any Disabilites or Restrictions on Persons of the Native Race to which Persons of European Birth or Descent would not also be subjected :

12. Altering in any way the Criminal Law of *New Zealand*, except so far as relates to the Trial and Punishment of such Offences as are now or may by the Criminal Law of *New Zealand* be punishable in a summary Way as aforesaid :

13. Regulating the Course of Inheritance of Real or Personal Property, or affecting the Law relating to Wills.

Though the Local Councils were not forbidden from legislating on subjects not specified above, the governor-in-council, retained power to annul the election of the local superintendent, to instruct him in his office, and finally within a limited time to "disallow" his and the local Council's acts.

Grave doubts were expressed at the time of the passage of the Constitutional Act, as to the wisdom shown by Parliament in adjusting the division of powers between the local and general governments,—a subject of great interest to us, in Canada. The late Mr. John Robert Godley, the founder of one of the Provinces, (Canterbury), in a lecture delivered at Lyttleton, in that Province, on the arrival of the new charter from England, thus expressed the views of himself and others, on this head:

I have said that the relation of British colonies to Parliament brings them into the first category of what I have called aggregate systems of government. The second category comprises those systems of government which are formed on the principle of Federation. In these it is not a supreme Central government that delegates certain limited functions to Local governments, but a number of independent and sovereign States agree for their mutual benefit to combine, and to delegate a certain portion of *their* sovereignty to a Central government. Of course it follows from this process that instead of, as in the former case, the Central government remaining supreme and permanent in all things over the Local governments, the latter retain in full integrity all the powers which they have not expressly delegated, and in respect of these powers are as completely sovereign and independent as they were before the union. Such were the principles on which in ancient times the Amphictyonic and Achean, and in modern times the German and Dutch Confederacies, were founded. Such, too, is the relation which subsists between the separate States of the American Union and the Federal government, and between the Cantons of Switzerland and the government of the Helvetic League. In framing the Constitution of this colony, to which physical circumstances as well as moral considerations, made the application of one or other of these systems desirable, it lay with Parliament to determine which of the two they would give it. Were they to treat the Central government as though it had been the original constituent authority, and to give it those paramount prevailing and controlling powers over the whole colony of New Zealand which Parliament itself possesses over the whole British Empire? Or were they to treat the provinces as integral independent units, and starting as it were from that idea, to make them give up only just so much governmental authority to the Central government as might be considered necessary for the general good retaining all powers not so expressly delegated?

I need not tell you that the former was the plan which the minister proposed and Parliament adopted. Your Constitution provides that the Central Legislature of New Zealand shall have an unlimited power of making laws for New Zealand, so far, that is, as is consistent with its subordination to the mother country. There are certain subjects enumerated which the Provincial Legislatures are not to touch, with which the Central Legislature therefore alone can deal; but there is no corresponding restriction on the powers of the Central government: on the contrary, it is enacted "that the laws made by the General Assembly shall control and supersede all laws in anywise repugnant thereto, which may have been made prior thereto by any Provincial Council, and any law made by any Provincial Council shall, so far as the same is repugnant to or inconsistent with any Act passed by the General Assembly, be null and void." Carrying out the same view, the Act makes all the legislation of the Provincial Councils to be subject to the governor's disallowance. It enables the governor to disallow also the election of the superintendent, and requires that the superintendent shall obey the governor's instructions implicitly with regard to the exercise of all his functions. Indeed the superintendent has no power conferred on him by the Act, except the nominal power which it hardly required the authority of Parliament to confer, of transmitting drafts of laws for the consideration of the Provincial Council, and of giving and withholding assent to Bills, in accordance with instructions from the governor. I will consider this part of my subject in relation first to the legislative, and next to the executive powers of the Central and the Provincial authorities respectively. Upon the first question, whether the Provincial Legislature should or should not have been made *by the Constitutional Act* independent of the Central Legislature, I do not feel so strongly as most of those with whom I generally agree. I attach, too, more importance than I think they do to the inconvenience and evils of having these islands cut up into six or eight petty states, with different codes of law, and perhaps different systems of government, and therefore it is with some hesitation that I have been led to advocate the complete municipal independence of the Provinces, especially as there is danger lest such unreserved independence tend to perpetuate the little jealousies and rivalries which the various circumstances of their respective origins have produced. On every account I look anxiously forward to the time when their complete amalgamation will be possible. I have no wish to see a hexarchy prolonged in a country the whole of which is of perfectly manageable dimensions, not larger than Great Britain and Ireland, or than many of the American States. The normal state of New Zealand ought, in my opinion, as regards this point, to be that of England, not of America. I see nothing which ought to prevent at any very distant time the Parliament of New Zealand legislating for all the islands; just as the Parliament of Great Britain legislates for Caithness and Cork, and that of New York for Long Island and Buffalo. The question between Federalism and unitarianism (if I may so call it) is in my mind entirely one of geography, where there are no essential differences of race, or other social peculiarities which forbid amalgamation. Unity is best where you can have it, and the tendency of things is towards making political unity more and more possible every year among peoples hitherto divided. Electricity and steam are the most powerful of political amalgamators; it is easier now to govern the Highlands and Connaught from the home secretary's office in Downing-street, than it formerly was to govern Devonshire and Northumberland; and I hope many of you will live to see the Bluff and the Bay of Islands brought as near to each other as John O'Groat's house and the Lizard.

Still feeling all this very strongly, I cannot see but that at present this colony is not fit for centralized government; not merely because communications are imperfect, but because you really cannot get people to make politics a profession, and to suspend a considerable part of their time at a distance from their homes. Nor are the people, I think, disposed or fitted to work together, as I trust they will be when they have mixed more with each other, and become more naturalized in their new homes. They would obviously prefer keeping apart, and managing each settlement its own affairs; and this is a feeling upon which certainly no force should be put. The popular instinct is likely to be right, and at any rate cannot be contended with. I am content, therefore, to acquiesce in what I see clearly the event will be—namely, the abdication by the General Assembly of as much of its functions as it can with decency and propriety abdicate, both in order to save its members the inconvenience of frequent and protracted sessions, and because their constituents will prefer to have the chief part of their affairs locally managed. The history of governments analogous to that of New Zealand shows almost invariably a constant growth of the central element, and I see little reason to suppose that New Zealand will be an exception to the rule. The reasons for this lie deep in the first principles of human nature; in its jealousy of external control, in its local attachments, its pride, its prejudices, its narrow-mindedness, its patriotism. Upon the same principle that a man is more attached to his family than his neighborhood, to his neighborhood than to the community at large, the people of each Confederated State are sure to feel a stronger bias towards the government of their own State than towards the Central government; and are sure to wish as much power as possible to be thrown into the hands of the former. There is no fear on that side of the question, except for one consideration, which I earnestly hope may prove temporary and evanescent. What I refer to is this: at present no doubt the struggle between the two will be apt to take more or less the form of a struggle between the mother country and the colonists, because every diminution of the power of the Central government will be of course so much taken from the power of the governor, who is an Imperial officer, and given to the superintendent, who is essentially a colonial officer; but I do not anticipate from that quarter any prolonged resistance to Provincial aggression. If the Central Assembly and the people generally desire to

D

throw more and more of the management of affairs into the hands of the Provinces, the mother country will soon, I think, get tired of interfering for the sake of preserving her indirect influence through the instrumentality of the Central government ; and, remember, there is no other obstacle to the will of the provincial constituencies. Their aggregate makes up the central constituency. It is not here, as it is, has been in many European countries, where the central power has encroached on the privileges of municipal bodies. In these latter cases, you will find that the central power has always rested on a different basis, generally the basis of a powerful monarchy ; while the municipalities were scattered and weak, and comprised a small proportion of the people. I repeat that in every case which I can remember of the same people choosing a central governing body, and local governing bodies, the local bodies have proved victors in the struggle which necessarily to some extent ensues. I am not, therefore, as some of my friends are, disposed to look with jealousy on the possibility of the Central Assembly wishing to retain too much power in its hands. I am more afraid of the provinces wishing to retain for an indefinite time ampler powers than will ultimately be consistent with the utmost development of the national greatness and prosperity of New Zealand.*

I cannot say, how much or how little of these commentaries have been fulfilled in the twelve years that have since elapsed. But it is gratifying, in either case to know, that despite of more than one native war, the population and material prosperity of the only federally governed colonies of Great Britain have gone on increasing, in an unprecedented ratio.

---

* Writings and speeches of John Robert Godley. Edited by James Edward Fitzgerald. Christ's Church, New Zealand, 1863, pp. 144-148

IX.—Conclusion.

Mr. Freeman, the Historian of the *Greek ·Federations*, concludes his volume by an eloquent exhortation in favor of the revival of that form of government among the Greeks of the present day. "One set of circumstances," he says, "points to Federal Union, another set of circumstances points to princely government. A monarchic Federation on such a scale has never yet existed, but it is not in itself at all contradictory to the Federal ideal."

We have in British America the same problem to solve that Mr. Freeman thus puts before the Greeks. To the vast majority of our population the monarchical idea is respectable if not venerable, is full of the promise of permanency, without being considered in any respect incompatible with the largest liberty. This vast majority, either born amidst or long accustomed to the greater equality of fortunes, and greater laxity of manners which characterize these, like all other American communities (when compared with European countries), have necessarily very decided democratic tendencies working within them. To regulate this two-fold movement of our public mind,—to see that freedom 'suffers nothing, while authority is exalted,—would seem to be our task, in the times on which we have fallen.

The reader of the previous pages will have observed one result of all the Federal forms of government which have hitherto prevailed in the world, that the jealous precautions taken by their founders, against the executive or central power, whether electoral or hereditary, have invariably defeated themselves. Whenever the executive class did not successfully usurp the place in the State which the contrivers of such fetters and restraints forbade them to aspire to, the whole Federal framework broke up in chaos. It was so in the Greek Confederacies; so in the Italian; so in the Netherlands. Switzerland, it is true, may be thought an exception,—but what a price has she not paid for executive impotency?

The United States Constitution of 1789, though a vast advance on the previous "Articles of Confederation," was not wholly free from this inherent vice. It was a Constitution made for times of peace and concord, and not to stand rough weather. And what have we seen? The only unwritten law of the Union,—the law inherent in all governments,—the law of self-preservation,—has overruled all other laws. The executive authority to save itself, and to save the Union, has been compelled to usurp those powers which the Constitution withheld, and to plead an inviolability from censure, pending the civil war, as extensive as most monarchs by "right divine," ever pretended to.

It may honestly be claimed, however, for all the Federal governments with which we have just renewed our acquaintance, that they were free governments; that they rested mainly on the *sensus communis* of the governed; that they secured internal peace,—and, therefore, were so far civilizers of men; that they promoted the useful and elegant arts; that they were nurseries of genius and public virtue; that they often averted invasion and war, by the imposing front they presented to external powers; that commerce, letters, and law, are deeply in their debt. Consolidated governments have their own merits, and boast their own achievements,—but so much as we have set down must be fairly credited to the Federal system. Although the great advances made, in all directions by the human mind, to which we have referred, *might* have been made in consolidated states, and under the most centralized systems, still the fact remains, that they *did* take place, under a combined provincial and metropolitan system of government. This is not the place to illustrate in detail this important truth; but though the writer may not at present enlarge upon its evidences, it is not the less worthy of the reader's most serious examination.

If it is reserved for the good people of these North American Provinces to establish in this age, for themselves and their posterity, principles of government at once permanent and progressive; a system strong and free; just but discriminating; stern to punish, ready to redress, and liberal to reward; the means of making up the public judgment as to the constitutional arrangements essential to such a system, are accessible enough. For two thousand years the human race have exhibited their political experiments in history; nor are the latest chapters of that history, written in our own language, among our next neighbors, descendants of the same ancestors as ourselves, the least instructive of the lessons which the teacher Time is prepared to unfold to us.

APPENDIX.

THE NEW ZEALAND CONSTITUTIONAL ACT, 15 & 16 VIC., CAP. LXXII.

An Act to grant a Representative Constitution to the Colony of *New Zealand.*

[30th *June,* 1852.]

' WHEREAS by an Act of the Session holden in the Third and Fourth
' Years of Her Majesty, Chapter Sixty-two, it was enacted, that
' it should be lawful for Her Majesty, by Letters Patent, to be from Time
' to Time issued under the Great Seal of the United Kingdom, to erect
' into a separate Colony or Colonies any Islands which then were or which
' thereafter might be comprised within and be Dependencies of the Co-
' lony of *New South Wales:* And whereas, in pursuance of the Powers in
' Her vested by the said Act, Her Majesty did, by certain Letters Patent
' under the Great Seal of the United Kingdom, bearing Date the Sixteenth
' Day of *November* in the Fourth Year of Her Reign, erect into a separate
' Colony the Islands of *New Zealand,* theretofore comprised within or
' Dependencies of the Colony of *New South Wales,* bounded as therein
' described, and the said Islands of *New Zealand* were thereby erected
' into a separate Colony accordingly ; and Her Majesty did by the said
' Letters Patent authorize the Governor for the Time being of the said
' Colony of *New Zealand* and certain other Persons to be a Legislative
' Council for such Colony, and to make Laws for the Peace, Order, and
' good Government thereof : And whereas by an Act of the Session
' holden in the Ninth and Tenth Years of Her Majesty, Chapter One
' hundred and three, the Act firstly herein recited, and all Charters,
' Letters Patent, Instructions, and Orders in Council made and issued
' in pursuance thereof, were repealed, abrogated, and annulled, so far as
' the same were repugnant to the Act now in recital, or any Letters
' Patent, Charters, Orders in Council, or Royal Instructions to be issued
' under the Authority thereof; and by the Act now in recital certain
' Powers for the Government of the said Islands were vested in Her
' Majesty, to be executed by Letters Patent under the Great Seal of the
' United Kingdom, or by Instructions under Her Majesty's Signet and

' Sign Manual, approved in Her Privy Council, and accompanying or
' referred to in such Letters Patent : And whereas, in pursuance of the
' said last-mentioned Act, Her Majesty did, by Letters Patent, bearing
' Date at *Westminster* the Twenty-third Day of *December* in the Tenth .
' Year of Her Reign, and by certain Instructions made and approved as
' required by such Act, and bearing even Date with and accompanying
' the said Letters Patent, execute certain of the Powers by such Act
' vested in Her Majesty for the better Government of the said Islands :
' And whereas by an Act of the Session holden in the Eleventh and
' Twelfth Years of Her Majesty, Chapter Five, so much of the said Act
' secondly herein recited, and the said Letters Patent and Instructions
' issued in pursuance thereof, as relates to the Constitution and Estab-
' lishment of two or more separate Assemblies within the said Islands,
' and of a General Assembly in and for the said Islands, was suspended
' for Five Years, unless Her Majesty, with the Advice of Her Privy
' Council, should direct the same to be carried into effect before the Expi-
' ration of that Period ; and by the Act now in recital the said firstly-
' recited Act, Letters Patent, and Instructions were revised for the time
' during which the said secondly recited Act, Letters Patent, and Instruc-
' tions were suspended as aforesaid ; and by the Act now in recital cer-
' tain Powers were vested respectively in the Governor-in-Chief of
' the said Islands and in such Governor and the Legislative Council
' thereof : And whereas it is expedient that further and better Provi-
' sion should be made for the Government of *New Zealand :*' Be it therefore enacted by the Queen's most Excellent Majesty, by and with the
Advice and Consent of the Lords Spiritual and Temporal, and Commons, in this present Parliament assembled, and by the Authority of the
same, as follows :

I. The said Acts, and all Charters, Letters Patent, Instructions, and
Orders in Council issued in pursuance thereof, shall be and the same are
hereby repealed, so far as the same are repugnant to or would prevent or
interfere with the Operation of this Act, or any Letters Patent or
Instructions to be issued under the Authority or in pursuance of this
Act : Provided nevertheless, that all Laws and Ordinances made and
Acts done under and in pursuance of the said recited Acts, and any
Charters, Letters Patent, Instructions, or Orders in Council issued in
pursuance thereof, shall continue as lawful, valid, and effectual as if
this Act had not been passed, save so far as any such Laws, Ordinances,
or Acts may be repugnant to or would prevent or interfere with the
Operation of this Act : Provided also, that, until the Expiration of the
Time or latest of the Times appointed for the Return of Writs for the
First Election of Members of the Provincial Councils of the Provinces
established by this Act, the existing Provincial Legislative Councils

shall continue to have and exercise all Rights, Jurisdiction, Powers, and Authorities which they would have had if this Act had not been passed ; and until the Expiration of the Time appointed for the Return of the Writs for the first Election of the Members of the House of Representatives to be constituted under this Act, the Legislative Council of *New Zealand* shall continue to have and exercise all Rights, Jurisdiction, Powers, and Authorities which such Legislative Council would have had if this Act had not been passed.

II. The following Provinces are hereby established in *New Zealand ;* namely, *Auckland, New Plymouth, Wellington, Nelson, Canterbury,* and *Otago ;* and the Limits of such several Provinces shall be fixed by Proclamation by the Governor as soon as conveniently may be after the Proclamation of this Act in *New Zealand.*

III. For each of the said Provinces hereby established, and for every Province hereafter to be established as hereinafter provided, there shall be a Superintendent and a Provincial Council, and the Provincial Council of each of the said Provinces hereby established shall consist of such Number of Members, not less than Nine, as the Governor shall by Proclamation direct and appoint.

IV. Upon or before the Issue of Writs for the First Election of Members of the Provincial Council for any Province established by or under this Act, the Persons duly qualified in each of the said Provinces to elect Members for the Provincial Councils as hereinafter mentioned shall elect a Superintendent of such Province ; and on the Termination of such Council by Expiration of the Period hereinafter fixed for its Continuance, or by the previous Dissolution thereof, the Persons qualified as aforesaid shall elect the same or some other Person to be Superintendent, and so on from Time to Time ; and every such Superintendent shall hold his Office until the Election of his Successor : Provided always, that it shall be lawful for the Governor of *New Zealand,* on behalf of Her Majesty, to disallow any such Election ; and if such Disallowance be signified by the Governor, under the Seal of *New Zealand,* to the Speaker of such Council, at any Time within Three Months after such Election, the Office of Superintendent shall become vacant ; and on any Vacancy occasioned by such Disallowance, or by the Death or Resignation of the Superintendent (such Resignation being accepted by the Governor on behalf of Her Majesty), a new Election shall in like Manner take place : Provided farther, that at any Time during the Continuance of the Office of any such Superintendent it shall be lawful for Her Majesty to remove him from such Office, on receiving an Address signed by the Majority of the Members of such Provincial Council praying for such Removal; and thereupon the like Proceedings shall be had as in the Case of any such Vacancy as above mentioned.

V. It shall be lawful for the Governor, by Proclamation, to constitute within each of the said Provinces hereby established convenient Electoral Districts for the Election of Members of the Provincial Council, and of the Superintendent, and to appoint and declare the Number of Members to be elected for each such District for the Provincial Council, and to make Provision for the Registration and Revision of Lists of all Persons qualified to vote at the Elections to be holden within such Districts, and for the appointing of Returning Officers, and for issuing, executing, and returning the necessary Writs for such Elections, and for taking the Poll thereat, and for determining the Validity of all disputed Returns, and otherwise for ensuring the orderly, effective, and impartial Conduct of such Elections; and in determining the Number and Extent of such Electoral Districts, and the Number of Members to be elected for each District, regard shall be had to the Number of Electors within the same, so that the Number of Members to be assigned to any One District may bear to the whole Number of the Members of the said Council, as nearly as may be, the same Proportion as the Number of Electors within such District shall bear to the whole Number of Electors within the Limits of the Province.

VI. Every Person within any Province hereby established or hereafter to be established who shall be legally qualified as an Elector, and duly registered as such, shall be qualified to be elected a Member of the Provincial Council thereof, or to be elected Superintendent thereof: Provided always, that it shall not be necessary that he reside or possess the Qualification in the particular District for which he may be elected to serve as a Member.

VII. The Members of every such Council shall be chosen by the Votes of the Inhabitants of the Province who may be qualified as hereinafter mentioned; that is to say, every Man of the Age of Twenty-one Years or upwards having a Freehold Estate in possession situate within the District for which the Vote is to be given of the clear Value of Fifty Pounds above all Charges and Incumbrances, and of or to which he has been seised or entitled, either at Law or in Equity, for at least Six Calendar Months next before the last Registration of Electors, or having a Leasehold Estate in possession situate within such District, of the clear annual Value of Ten Pounds, held upon a Lease which at the Time of such Registration shall have not less than Three Years to run, or having a Leasehold Estate so situate, and of such Value as aforesaid of which he has been in possession for Three Years or upwards next before such Registration, or being a Householder within such District occupying a Tenement within the Limits of a Town (to be proclaimed as such by the Governor for the purposes of this Act) of the clear annual Value of Ten Pounds, or without the Limits of a Town of the clear annual

Value of Five Pounds, and having resided therein Six Calendar Months next before such Registration as aforesaid, shall, if duly registered, be entitled to vote at the Election of a Member or Members for the District.

VIII. Provided always, That no Person shall be entitled to vote at any such Election who is an Alien, or who at any Time theretofore shall have been attainted or convicted of any Treason, Felony, or infamous Offence within any Part of Her Majesty's Dominions, unless he shall have received a free pardon, or shall have undergone the sentence or punishment to which he shall have been adjudged for such Offence.

IX. It shall be lawful for any Member of any Provincial Council, by Writing under his Hand, addressed to the Superintendent of the Province, to resign his Seat in the said Council; and upon the Receipt by the Superintendent of such Resignation the Seat of such Member shall become vacant.

X. If any Member of any Provincial Council shall for Two successive Sessions of such Council fail to give his Attendance therein, or shall become bankrupt, or shall become an Insolvent Debtor within the Meaning of the Laws relating to Insolvent Debtors, or shall become a public Defaulter, or be attainted of Treason, or be convicted of Felony or any infamous Offence, his Seat in such Council shall thereupon become vacant.

XI. Any Question which shall arise respecting any Vacancy in a Provincial Council on occasion of any of the Matters aforesaid shall be heard and determined by such Council, on such Question being referred to them for that Purpose by the Superintendent of the Province, and not otherwise.

XII. Whenever it shall be established to the satisfaction of the Superintendent that the Seat of any Member of the Provincial Council has become vacant, the Superintendent shall forthwith issue a Writ for the Election of a new Member to serve in the Place so vacated, during the Remainder of the Term of the Continuance of such Council, and no longer.

XIII. Every Provincial Council shall continue for the Period of Four Years from the Day of the Return of the Writs for choosing the same, and no longer; Provided always, that it shall be lawful for the Governor, by Proclamation or otherwise, sooner to dissolve the same, whenever he shall deem it expedient so to do.

XIV. The Governor shall cause the First Writs for the Election of Members of the Provincial Council of every Province hereby established to be issued at some time not later than Six Calendar Months next after the Proclamation of this Act in *New Zealand;* and upon the Expiration of the said Period of the Continuance of any Provincial Council, or upon the Previous Dissolution thereof, the Governor shall cause Writs to be issued for the Election of Members of the ensuing Council.

XV. It shall be lawful for the Superintendent by Proclamation in the Government Gazette, to fix such Place or Places within the Limits of the Province, and such Times for holding the first and every other Session of the Provincial Council, as he may think fit, and from Time to Time, in manner aforesaid, to alter and vary such Times and Places as he may judge advisable, and most consistent with general Convenience.

XVI. It shall be lawful for the Superintendent to prorogue such Council from Time to Time whenever he shall deem it expedient so to do.

XVII. Provided always, That there shall be a Session of every Provincial Council once at least in every Year, so that a greater Period than Twelve Calendar Months shall not intervene between the last Sitting of the Council in One Session and the First Sitting of the Council in the next Session.

XVIII. It shall be lawful for the Superintendent of each Province, with the Advice and Consent of the Provincial Council thereof, to make and ordain all such Laws and Ordinances (except and subject as hereinafter mentioned) as may be required for the Peace, Order, and good Government of such Province, provided that the same be not repugnant to the Law of *England*.

XIX. It shall not be lawful for the Superintendent and Provincial Council to make or ordain any Law or Ordinance for any of the Purposes hereinafter mentioned; (that is to say,)

1. The Imposition or Regulation of Duties of Customs to be imposed on the Importation or Exportation of any Goods at any Port or Place in the Province :

2. The Establishment or Abolition of any Court of Judicature of Civil or Criminal Jurisdiction, except Courts for trying and punishing such Offences as by the Law of *New Zealand* are or may be made punishable in a summary Way, or altering the Constitution, Jurisdiction, or Practice of any such Court, except as aforesaid :

3. Regulating any of the current Coin, or the Issue of any Bills, Notes, or other Paper Currency :

4. Regulating the Weights and Measures to be used in the Province or in any Part thereof :

5. Regulating the Post Offices and the Carriage of Letters within the Province :

6. Establishing, altering, or repealing Laws relating to Bankruptcy or Insolvency :

7. The Erection and Maintenance of Beacons and Lighthouses on the Coast :

8. The imposition of any Dues or other Charges on Shipping at any Port or Harbour in the Province :

9. Regulating Marriages:

10. Affecting Lands of the Crown, or Lands to which the Title of the Aboriginal native Owners has never been extinguished:

11. Inflicting any Disabilities or Restrictions on Persons of the Native Race to which Persons of European Birth or Descent would not also be subjected:

12. Altering in any way the Criminal Law of *New Zealand*, except so far as relates to the Trial and Punishment of such Offences as are now or may by the Criminal Law of *New Zealand* be punishable in a summary Way as aforesaid:

13. Regulating the Course of Inheritance of Real or Personal Property, or affecting the Law relating to Wills.

XX. Every Provincial Council shall immediately on their First Meeting, and before proceeding to the Despatch of any other Business, elect One of their Members to be the Speaker thereof, during the Continuance of such Council, which Election being confirmed by the Superintendent shall be valid and effectual; and in case of Vacancy in the said Office by Death, Resignation, or otherwise, then and so often as the same shall happen the Election shall be repeated and confirmed as aforesaid.

XXI. The Speaker of each Provincial Council shall preside at the Meetings of such Council; but in his Absence some Member elected by the Council shall preside.

XXII. No Provincial Council shall be competent to the Despatch of any Business, unless One Third of the whole Number of Members be present.

XXIII. All Questions which shall arise in any such Council shall be decided by the Majority of Votes of the Members present other than the Speaker or presiding Member; but in all Cases wherein the Votes shall be equal, the Speaker or presiding Member shall have a Casting Vote.

XXIV. Every Provincial Council at their First Meeting, and from Time to Time afterwards, as Occasion may require, shall prepare and adopt such Standing Rules and Orders as may be best adapted for the orderly Conduct of the Business of such Council, which Rules and Orders shall be laid before the Superintendent, and being by him approved shall then become binding and in force.

XXV. It shall not be lawful for any Provincial Council to pass, or for the Superintendent to assent to, any Bill appropriating any Money to the Public Service, unless the Superintendent shall first have recommended to the Council to make Provision for the specific Service to which such Money is to be appropriated; and no such Money shall be issued or be made issuable, except by Warrants to be granted by the Superintendent.

XXVI. It shall be lawful for the Superintendent to transmit to the

Provincial Council, for their Consideration, the Drafts of any such Laws or Ordinances as it may appear to him desirable to introduce, and all such Drafts shall be taken into consideration in such convenient Manner as in and by such Rules and Orders as aforesaid shall be in that Behalf provided.

XXVII. Every Bill passed by the Provincial Council shall be presented to the Superintendent for the Governor's Assent, and the Superintendent shall declare, according to his Discretion, (but subject nevertheless to the Provisions herein contained and to such Instructions as may from Time to Time be given him by the Governor,) that he assents to such Bill on behalf of the Governor, or that he withholds the Assent of the Governor, or that he reserves such Bill for the Signification of the Governor's Pleasure thereon; provided always, that it shall and may be lawful for the Superintendent, before declaring his Pleasure in regard to any Bill so presented to him, to make such Amendments in such Bill as he thinks needful or expedient, and to return such Bill with such Amendments to such Council, and the Consideration of such Amendments by such Council shall take place in such convenient Manner as shall in and by the Rules and Orders aforesaid be in that Behalf provided; provided also, that all Bills altering or affecting the Extent of the several Electoral Districts which shall be represented in the Provincial Council, or establishing new or other such Electoral Districts, or altering the Number of the Members of such Council to be chosen by the said Districts respectively, or altering the Number of the Members of such Council, or altering the Limits of any Town or establishing any new Town, shall be so reserved as aforesaid.

XXVIII. Whenever any Bill shall have been assented to by the Superintendent as aforesaid, the Superintendent shall forthwith transmit to the Governor an authentic Copy thereof.

XXIX. It shall be lawful for the Governor at any Time within Three Months after any such Bill shall have been received by him to declare by Proclamation his Disallowance of such Bill, and such Disallowance shall make void and annul the same from and after the Day of the Date of such Proclamation or any subsequent Day to be named therein.

XXX. No Bill which shall be reserved for the Signification of the Assent of the Governor shall have any Force or Authority within the Province until the Superintendent shall signify either by Speech or Message to the Provincial Council, or by Proclamation in the Government Gazette, that such Bill has been laid before the Governor, and that the Governor has assented to the same; and an Entry shall be made in the Journals of the Provincial Council of every such Speech, Message, or Proclamation, and a Duplicate thereof, duly attested, shall be delivered to the Registrar of the Supreme Court, or other proper Officer, to be kept among the Records of the Province; and no Bill which shall be so reserved as aforesaid shall have any Force or Authority within the Province unless the Assent of the Governor thereto shall have been so signified as aforesaid within Three Months next after the Day on which such Bill shall have been presented to the Superintendent for the Governor's Assent.

XXXI. It shall be lawful for the Governor from Time to Time to transmit to the Superintendent of any Province, for his Guidance in assenting to or withholding Assent from Bills, or reserving the same for the Signification of the Governor's Pleasure thereon, such Instructions as to the Governor shall seem fit, and it shall be the Duty of the Superintendent to act in obedience to such Instructions.

XXXII. There shall be within the Colony of *New Zealand* a General Assembly, to consist of the Governor, a Legislative Council, and House of Representatives.

XXXIII. For constituting the Legislative Council of *New Zealand* it shall be lawful for Her Majesty, before the Time to be appointed for the First Meeting of the General Assembly, by an Instrument under Her Royal Sign Manual, to authorize the Governor in Her Majesty's Name to summon to the said Legislative Council such Persons, being not less in Number than Ten, as Her Majesty shall think fit; and it shall also be lawful for Her Majesty from Time to Time in like Manner to authorize the Governor to summon to the said Legislative Council such other Person or Persons as Her Majesty shall think fit, either for supplying any Vacancy or Vacancies or otherwise, and every Person who shall be so summoned shall thereby become a Member of the said Legislative Council: Provided always, that no Person shall be summoned to such Legislative Council who shall not be of the full Age of Twenty-one Years, and a natural born Subject of Her Majesty, or a Subject of Her Majesty naturalized by Act of Parliament, or by an Act of the Legislature of *New Zealand*.

XXXIV. Every Member of the Legislative Council of *New Zealand* shall hold his Seat therein for the Term of his Life, subject nevertheless to the Provisions hereinafter contained for vacating the same.

XXXV. It shall be lawful for any Member of the said Legislative Council, by Writing under his Hand addressed to the Governor, to resign his Seat in the said Council, and upon such Resignation and Acceptance thereof by the Governor the Seat of such Member shall become vacant.

XXXVI. If any Legislative Councillor of *New Zealand* shall for Two successive Sessions of the General Assembly, without the Permission of Her Majesty or of the Governor, signified by the said Governor to the Legislative Council, fail to give his Attendance in the said Legislative Council, or shall take any Oath or make any Declaration or Acknowledgment of Allegiance, Obedience, or Adherence to any Foreign Prince or Power, or shall do, concur in, or adopt any Act whereby he may become a Subject or Citizen of any Foreign State or Power, or become entitled to the Rights, Privileges or Immunities of a Subject or Citizen of any Foreign State or Power, or shall become bankrupt, or shall become an Insolvent Debtor within the Meaning of the Laws relating to Insolvent Debtors, or shall become a public Defaulter, or be attainted of Treason, or be convicted of Felony or any infamous Crime, his Seat in such Council shall thereby become vacant.

XXXVII. Any Question which shall arise respecting any Vacancy in the said Legislative Council on occasion of any of the Matters aforesaid, shall be referred by the Governor to the said Legislative Council, to be by the said Legislative Council heard and determined : Provided always, that it shall be lawful, either for the Person respecting whose Seat such Question shall have arisen, or for Her Majesty's Attorney General for *New Zealand* on Her Majesty's Behalf, to appeal from the Determination of the said Council in such Case to Her Majesty, and the Judgment of Her Majesty given with the Advice of Her Privy Council thereon shall be final and conclusive to all Intents and Purposes.

XXXVIII. The Governor shall have Power and Authority from Time to Time to appoint One Member of the said Legislative Council to be Speaker of such Council, and to remove him and appoint another in his Stead.

XXXIX. The Presence of at least Five Members of the said Legislative Council, including the Speaker, shall be necessary to constitute a Meeting for the Exercise of its Powers ; and all Questions which shall arise in the said Legislative Council shall be decided by a Majority of Votes of the Members present other than the Speaker, and when the Votes shall be equal the Speaker shall have the Casting Vote.

XL. For the Purpose of constituting the House of Representatives of *New Zealand* it shall be lawful for the Governor, within the Time hereinafter mentioned, and thereafter from Time to Time as Occasion shall require, by Proclamation in Her Majesty's Name, to summon and call together a House of Representatives in and for *New Zealand*, such House of Representatives to consist of such Number of Members, not more than Forty-two nor less than Twenty-four, as the Governor shall by Proclamation in that Behalf direct and appoint; and every such House of Representatives shall, unless the General Assembly shall be sooner dissolved, continue for the Period of Five Years from the Day of the Return of the Writs for choosing such House, and no longer.

XLI. It shall be lawful for the Governor by Proclamation to constitute within *New Zealand* convenient Electoral Districts for the Election of Members of the said House of Representatives, and to appoint and declare the Number of such Members to be elected for each such District, and to make Provision (so far as may be necessary beyond the Provision which may be made for the like Purposes in relating to Elections for Provincial Councils) for the Registration and Revision of Lists of all Persons qualified to vote at the Elections to be holden within such Districts, and also Provision for the appointing of Returning Officers, and for issuing, executing, and returning the necessary Writs for Elections of Members of the House of Representatives, and for taking the Poll thereat, and otherwise for ensuring the orderly, effective and impartial Conduct of such Elections; and in determining the Number and Extent of such Electoral Districts, and the Number of Members to be elected for each District, regard shall be had to the Number of Electors within the same, so that the Number of Members to be assigned to any One District may bear to the whole Number of the Members of the House of Representatives, as nearly as may be, the same Proportion as the Number of Electors within such District shall bear to the whole Number of Electors in *New Zealand.*

XLII. The Members of the said House of Representatives to be chosen in every Electoral District appointed for that Purpose shall be chosen by the Votes of the Inhabitants of *New Zealand* who shall possess within such District the like Qualifications which, when possessed within an Electoral District appointed for the Election of Members of a Provincial Council, would entitle Inhabitants of the Province to vote in the Election of Members of the Provincial Council thereof, and who shall be duly registered as Electors; and every Person legally qualified as such Elector shall be qualified to be elected a Member of the said House.

XLIII. The Governor shall cause the First Writs for the Election of Members of the said House of Representatives to be issued at some Time not later than Six Calendar Months next after the Proclamation of this Act in *New Zealand;* and upon the Expiration of the said Period of the Continuance of the House of Representatives, or upon the previous Determination of such House by the Dissolution of the General Assembly, the Governor shall cause Writs to be issued for the Election of Members of the ensuing House of Representatives.

XLIV. The General Assembly of *New Zealand* shall be holden at any Place and Time within *New Zealand,* which the Governor shall from Time to Time by Proclamation for that Purpose appoint; and the Time so to be appointed for the first holding of such General Assembly shall be as soon as conveniently may be after the Return of the First Writs for the Election of Members of the said House of Representatives; and the Governor may at his Pleasure prorogue or dissolve the General Assembly.

XLV. The said House of Representatives shall, until Provision be otherwise made in that Behalf by Law, be Judges, without Appeal, of the Validity of the Election of each Member thereof.

XLVI. No Member of the said Legislative Council or House of Representatives shall be permitted to sit or vote therein until he shall have taken and subscribed the following Oath before the Governor, or before some Person or Persons authorized by him to administer such Oath :

' I *A.B.* do sincerely promise and swear, That I will be faithful and bear true Allegiance to Her Majesty Queen *Victoria*.

' So help me GOD.'

XLVII. Every Person authorized by Law to make his solemn Affirmation or Declaration instead of taking an Oath may make such Affirmation or Declaration in lieu of the said Oath.

XLVIII. The said House of Representatives shall immediately on their first Meeting proceed to the Choice of One of their Members as their Speaker during the continuance of the said House, which Choice, being confirmed by the Governor, shall be valid and effectual ; and in case of Vacancy of the office by Death, Resignation, or otherwise, then and so often as the same shall happen, the Choice shall be repeated and confirmed as aforesaid.

XLIX. It shall be lawful for any Member of the House of Representatives, by Writing under his Hand addressed to the Speaker of the said House, to resign his Seat in the said House, and upon such Resignation the Seat of such Member shall become vacant.

L. If any Member of the said House of Representatives shall for One whole Session of the General Assembly, without the Permission of such House, fail to give his Attendance in the said House, or shall take any Oath, or make any Declaration or Acknowledgment of Allegiance, Obedience, or Adherence to any Foreign Prince or Power, or do or concur in or adopt any Act whereby he may become a Subject or Citizen of any Foreign State or Power, or become entitled to the Rights, Privileges, or Immunities of a Subject of any Foreign State or Power, or shall become bankrupt, or shall become an Insolvent Debtor within the Meaning of the Laws relating to Insolvent Debtors, or shall become a public Defaulter, or be attainted of Treason, or be convicted of Felony or any infamous Crime, his Seat in such House shall thereby become vacant.

LI. When and so often as a Vacancy shall occur as aforesaid in any Seat in the said House of Representatives, it shall and may be lawful for such House to address the Governor, stating the Existence of such Vacancy and the cause thereof, and the Governor, upon receiving such Address, shall cause a Writ to be issued for supplying such Vacancy.

LII. The said Legislative Council and House of Representatives at the First Sitting of each respectively, and from Time to Time afterwards as there shall be Occasion, shall prepare and adopt such Standing Rules and Orders as shall appear to the said Council and House of Representatives respectively best adapted for the orderly Conduct of the Business of such Council and House respectively, and for the Manner in which such Council and House respectively shall be presided over in case of the Absence of the Speaker, and for the Mode in which such Council and House shall confer, correspond, and communicate with each other relative to Votes or Bills passed by or pending in such Council and House respectively, and for the Manner in which Notices of Bills, Resolutions, and other Business intended to be submitted to such Council and House respectively at any Session thereof may be published in the Government Gazette or otherwise for general Information for some convenient Space or Time before the Meeting of such Council and House respectively, and for the proper framing, entitling, and numbering of the Bills to be introduced into and passed by the said Council and House of Representatives, all of which Rules and Orders shall by such Council and House respectively be laid before the Governor, and being by him approved shall become binding and of force, but subject nevertheless to the Confirmation or Disallowance of Her Majesty in manner hereinafter provided respecting the Acts to be made by the Governor with the Advice and Consent of the said Legislative Council and House of Representatives ; provided that no such Rule or Order shall be of force to subject any Person, not being a Member or Officer of the Council or House to which it relates, to any Pain, Penalty, or Forfeiture.

LIII. It shall be competent to the said General Assembly (except and subject as hereinafter mentioned) to make Laws for the Peace, Order, and good Government of *New Zealand*, provided that no such Laws be repugnant to the Law of *England;* and the Laws so to be made by the said General Assembly shall control and supersede any Laws or Ordinances in anywise repugnant thereto which may have been made or ordained prior thereto by any Provincial Council; and any Law or Ordinance made or ordained by any Provincial Council in pursuance of the Authority hereby conferred upon it, and on any Subject whereon under such Authority as aforesaid it is entitled to legislate, shall, so far as the same is repugnant to or inconsistent with any Act passed by the General Assembly, be null and void.

LIV. It shall not be lawful for the House of Representatives or the Legislative Council to pass, or for the Governor to assent to, any Bill appropriating to the Public Service any Sum of Money from or out of Her Majesty's Revenue within *New Zealand*, unless the Governor on Her Majesty's Behalf shall first have recommended to the House of Representatives to make Provision for the specific Public Service towards which such Money is to be appropriated, and (save as herein otherwise provided) no Part of Her Majesty's Revenue within *New Zealand* shall be issued except in pursuance of Warrants under the Hand of the Governor directed to the public Treasurer thereof.

LV. It shall and may be lawful for the Governor to transmit by Message to either the said Legislative Council or the said House of Representatives for their Consideration the Drafts of any Laws which it may appear to him desirable to introduce, and all such Drafts shall be taken into consideration in such convenient Manner as shall in and by the Rules and Orders aforesaid be in that Behalf provided.

LVI. Whenever any Bill which has been passed by the said Legislative Council and House of Representatives shall be presented for Her Majesty's Assent to the Governor, he shall declare according to his Discretion, but subject nevertheless to the Provisions contained in this Act and to such Instructions as may from Time to Time be given in that Behalf by Her Majesty, Her Heirs or Successors, that he assents to such Bill in Her Majesty's Name, or that he refuses his assent to such Bill, or that he reserves such Bill for the Signification of Her Majesty's Pleasure thereon ; provided always, that it shall and may be lawful for the Governor, before declaring his Pleasure in regard to any Bill so presented to him, to make such Amendments in such Bill as he things needful or expedient, and by Message to return such Bill with such Amendments to the Legislative Council or the House of Representatives as he shall think the more fitting, and the Consideration of such Amendments by the said Council and House respectively shall take place in such convenient Manner as shall in and by the Rules and Orders aforesaid be in that Behalf provided.

LVII. It shall be lawful for Her Majesty, with the Advice of Her Privy Council, or under Her Majesty's Signet and Sign Manual, or through One of Her Principal Secretaries of State, from Time to Time to convey to the Governor of *New Zealand* such Instructions as to Her Majesty shall seem meet, for the Guidance of such Governor, for the Exercise of the Powers hereby vested in him of assenting to, or dissenting from, or for reserving for the Signification of Her Majesty's Pleasure, Bills to be passed by the said Legislative Council and House of Representatives; and it shall be the Duty of such Governor to act in obedience to such Instructions.

LVIII. Whenever any Bill which shall have been presented for Her Majesty's Assent to the Governor shall by such Governor have been assented to in Her Majesty's Name, he shall by the first convenient Opportunity transmit to One of Her Majesty's Principal Secretaries of State an authentic Copy of such Bill so assented to ; and it shall be lawful, at any Time within Two Years after such Bill shall have been received by the Secretary of State, for Her Majesty, by Order in Council, to declare

Her Disallowance of such Bill ; and such Disallowance, together with a Certificate under the Hand and Seal of the Secretary of State certifying the Day on which such Bill was received as aforesaid, being signified by the Governor to the said Legislative Council and House of Representatives by Speech or Message, or by Proclamation in the Government Gazette, shall make void and annul the same from and after the Day of such Signification.

LIX. No Bill which shall be reserved for the Signification of Her Majesty's Pleasure thereon shall have any Force or Authority within *New Zealand* until the Governor shall signify, either by Speech or Message to the said Legislative Council and House of Representatives, or by Proclamation, that such Bill has been laid before Her Majesty in Council, and that Her Majesty has been pleased to assent to the same ; and an Entry shall be made in the Journals of the said Legislative Council and House of Representatives of every such Speech, Message, or Proclamation, and a Duplicate thereof, duly attested, shall be delivered to the Registrar of the Supreme Court, or other proper Officer, to be kept among the Records of *New Zealand ;* and no Bill which shall be so reserved as aforesaid shall have any Force or Authority within *New Zealand,* unless Her Majesty's Assent thereto shall have been so signified as aforesaid within the Space of Two Years from the Day on which such Bill shall have been presented for Her Majesty's Assent to the Governor as aforesaid.

LX. The Governor shall cause every Act of the said General Assembly which he shall have assented to in Her Majesty's Name to be printed in the Government Gazette for general Information, and such Publication by such Governor of any such Act shall be deemed to be in Law the Promulgation of the same.

LXI. It shall not be lawful for the said General Assembly to levy any Duty upon Articles imported for the Supply of Her Majesty's Land or Sea Forces, or to levy any Duty, impose any Prohibition or Restriction, or grant any Exemptions, Bounty, Drawback, or other Privilege upon the Importation or Exportation of any Articles, or to impose any Dues or Charges upon Shipping contrary to or at variance with any Treaty or Treaties concluded by Her Majesty with any Foreign Power.

LXII. The Governor is hereby authorized and required to pay out of the Revenue arising from Taxes, Duties, Rates, and Imports levied under any Act or Acts of the said General Assembly, and from the Disposal of Waste Lands of the Crown, all the Costs, Charges, and Expenses incident to the Collection, Management, and Receipt thereof; also to pay out of the said Revenue arising from the Disposal of Waste Lands of the Crown such Sums as may become payable under the Provisions hereinafter contained for or on account of the Purchase of Land from aboriginal Natives, or the Release or Extinguishment of their Rights in any Land, and such Sums as may become payable to the *New Zealand* Company under the Provisions of this Act in respect of the Sale or Alienation of Land : Provided always, that full and particular Accounts of all such Disbursements shall from Time to Time be laid before the said Legislative Council and House of Representatives.

LXIII. All Costs, Charges, and Expenses of or incident to the Collection, Management, and Receipt of Duties of Import and Export shall be regulated and audited in such Manner as shall be directed by the Commissioners of Her Majesty's Treasury of the United Kingdom 'of' *Great Britain* and *Ireland*, and all such Costs, Charges, and Expenses in relation to other Branches of the said Revenue shall be regulated and audited in such Manner as shall be directed by Laws of the said General Assembly.

LXIV. There shall be payable to Her Majesty, every Year, out of the Revenue arising from such Taxes, Duties, Rates, and Imports, and from the Disposal of such Waste Lands of the Crown in *New Zealand*, the several Sums mentioned in the Schedule to this Act ; such several Sums to be paid for defraying the Expenses of the Services and Purposes mentioned in such Schedule, and to be issued by the Treasurer of *New Zealand* in discharge of such Warrants as shall be from Time to Time directed to him under the Hand and Seal of the Governor ; and the said Treasurer shall account to Her Majesty for the same through the Commissioners of Her Majesty's Treasury of the United Kingdom of *Great Britain* and *Ireland*, in such Manner and Form as Her Majesty shall be graciously pleased to direct.

LXV. It shall be lawful for the General Assembly of *New Zealand*, by any Act or Acts, to alter all or any of the Sums mentioned in the said Schedule, and the Appropriation of such Sums to the Services and Purposes therein mentioned ; but every Bill which shall be passed by the said Legislative Council and House of Representatives altering the Salary of the Governor, or altering the Sum described as for native Purposes, shall be reserved for the Signification of Her Majesty's Pleasure thereon, and until and subject to such alteration by Act or Acts as aforesaid the Salaries of the Governor and Judges shall be those respectively set against their several Offices in the said Schedule ; and Accounts in detail of the Expenditure of the several Sums for the Time being appropriated under this Act, or such Act or Acts as aforesaid of the said General Assembly, to the several Services and Purposes mentioned in the said Schedule, shall be laid before the said Legislative Council and House of Representatives within Thirty Days next after the Beginning of the Session after such Expenditure shall have been made : Provided always, that it shall not be lawful for the said General Assembly, by any such Act as aforesaid, to make any Diminution in the Salary of any Judge to take effect during the Continuance in Office of any Person being such Judge at the Time of the passing of such Act.

LXVI. After and subject to the Payments to be made under the Provisions hereinbefore contained, all the Revenue arising from Taxes, Duties, Rates, and Imposts levied in virtue of any Act of the General Assembly, and from the Disposal of Waste Lands of the Crown, under any such Act made in pursuance of the Authority herein contained, shall be subject to be appropriated to such specific Purposes as by any Act of the said General Assembly shall be prescribed in that Behalf; and the Surplus of such Revenue which shall not be appropriated as aforesaid shall be divided among the several Provinces for the Time being established in *New Zealand* under or by virtue of this Act, in the like Proportions as the gross Proceeds of the said Revenue shall have arisen therein respectively, and shall be paid over to the respective Treasuries of such Provinces for the public Uses thereof, and shall be subject to the Appropriation of the respective Provincial Councils of such Provinces.

LXVII. It shall be lawful for the said General Assembly, by any Act or Acts, from Time to Time, to establish new Electoral Districts for the Purpose of electing Members of the said House of Representatives, to alter the Boundaries of Electoral Districts for the Time being existing for such Purposes, to alter and appoint the Number of Members to be chosen for such Districts, to increase the whole Number of Members of the said House of Representatives, and to alter and regulate the Appointment of Returning Officers, and make Provision in such Manner as they may deem expedient for the Issue and Return of Writs for the Election of the Members of such House, and the Time and Place of holding such Elections, and for the Determination of contested Elections for such House.

LXVIII. It shall be lawful for the said General Assembly, by any Act or Acts, to alter from Time to Time any Provisions of this Act and any Laws for the Time being in force concerning the Election of Members of the said House of Representatives, and the Qualification of Electors and Members; provided that every Bill for any of such Purposes shall be reserved for the Signification of Her Majesty's Pleasure thereon, and a Copy of such Bill shall be laid before both Houses of Parliament for the Space of Thirty Days at the least before Her Majesty's Pleasure thereon shall be signified.

LXIX. It shall be lawful for the said General Assembly, by any Act or Acts from Time to Time, to constitute new Provinces in *New Zealand*, to direct and appoint the Number of Members of which the Provincial Councils thereof shall consist, and to alter the Boundaries of any Provinces for the Time being existing, and to alter the Provisions of this Act and any Laws for the Time being in force respecting the Election of Members of the Provincial Councils, the Powers of such Councils, and the Distribution of the said surplus Revenue between the several Provinces of *New Zealand;* Provided always, that any Bill for any of the said Purposes shall be reserved for the Signification of Her Majesty's Pleasure thereon.

LXX. It shall be lawful for Her Majesty, in and by any Letters Patent to be issued under the Great Seal of the United Kingdom, from Time to Time, to constitute and establish within any District or Districts of *New Zealand* One or more Municipal Corporation or Corporations, and to grant to any such Corporation all or any of the Powers which, in pursuance of the Statutes in that Behalf made and provided, it is competent to Her Majesty to grant to the Inhabitants of any Town or Borough in *England* and *Wales* incorporated in virtue of such Statutes or any of them, and to qualify and restrict the Exercise of any such Powers in such and the same Manner as, by the Statutes aforesaid or any of them, Her Majesty may qualify or restrict the Exercise of any such Powers as aforesaid in *England*: Provided always, that all Provisions of any such Letters Patent, and all Bye-laws or Regulations made by any such Corporation, shall be subject to Alteration or Repeal by any Ordinance or Act of the Provincial Council for the Province in which any such Corporation may be established, or of the General Assembly, according to their respective Powers hereinbefore declared.

LXXI. And whereas it may be expedient that the Laws, Customs, and Usages of the aboriginal or native Inhabitants of *New Zealand*, so far as they are not repugnant to the general Principles of Humanity, should for the present be maintained for the Government of themselves, in all their Relations to and Dealing with each other, and that particular Districts should be set apart within which such Laws, Customs, or Usages should be so observed:

It shall be lawful for Her Majesty, by any Letters Patent to be issued under the Great Seal of the United Kingdom, from Time to Time to make Provision for the Purposes aforesaid, any Repugnancy of any such native Laws, Customs, or Usages to the Law of *England*, or to any Law, Statute, or Usage in force in *New Zealand*, or in any part thereof, in anywise notwithstanding.

LXXII. Subject to the Provisions herein contained, it shall be lawful for the said General Assembly to make Laws for regulating the Sale, Letting, Disposal, and Occupation of the Waste Lands of the Crown in *New Zealand;* and all Lands wherein the Title of Natives shall be extinguished as hereinafter mentioned, and all such other Lands as are described in an Act of the Session holden in the Tenth and Eleventh

Years of Her Majesty, Chapter One hundred and twelve, to promote Colonization in *New Zealand*, and to authorize a Loan to the *New Zealand* Company, as Demesne Lands of the Crown, shall be deemed and taken to be Waste Lands of the Crown within the Meaning of this Act: Provided always, that subject to the said Provisions, and until the said General Assembly shall otherwise enact, it shall be lawful for Her Majesty to regulate such Sale, Letting, Disposal, and Occupation by Instructions to be issued under the Signet and Royal Sign Manual.

LXXIII. It shall not be lawful for any Person other than Her Majesty, Her Heirs or Successors, to purchase or in anywise acquire or accept from the aboriginal Natives Land of or belonging to or used or occupied by them in common as Tribes or Communities, or to accept any Release or Extinguishment of the Rights of such aboriginal Natives in any such Land as aforesaid; and no Conveyance or Transfer, or Agreement for the Conveyance or Transfer of any such Land, either in perpetuity or for any Term or Period, either absolutely or conditionally, and either in Property or by way of Lease or Occupancy; and no such Release or Extinguishment as aforesaid, shall be of any Validity or Effect unless the same be made to, or entered into with, and accepted by Her Majesty, Her Heirs or Successors: Provided always, that it shall be lawful for Her Majesty, Her Heirs and Successors, by Instructions under the Signet and Royal Sign Manual, or signified through One of Her Majesty's Principal Secretaries of State, to delegate Her Powers of accepting such Conveyances or Agreements, Releases or Relinquishments, to the Governor of *New Zealand*, or the Superintendent of any Province, within the limits of such Province, and to prescribe or regulate the Terms on which such Conveyances or Agreements, Releases, or Extinguishments shall be accepted.

LXXIV. And whereas under and by virtue of the said last mentioned Act, and of a Notice given on the Fourth Day of *July* One thousand eight hundred and fifty by the *New Zealand* Company in pursuance of such Act, the Sum of Two hundred and sixty-eight thousand three hundred and seventy Pounds Fifteen Shillings, with Interest after the yearly Rate of Three Pounds Ten Shillings *per Centum* upon the said Sum, or so much thereof as shall from Time to Time remain unpaid, is charged upon and payable to the *New Zealand* Company out of the Proceeds of the Sales of the Demesne Lands of the Crown in *New Zealand*:

In respect of all Sales or other Alienations of any Waste Lands of the Crown in *New Zealand* in Fee Simple or for any less Estate or Interest (except by way of Licence for Occupation for pastoral Purposes for any Term of Years not exceeding Seven, and not containing any Contract for the Renewal of the same, or for a further Estate, Interest, or Licence, or by way of Reservation of such Lands as may be required for public Roads or other internal Communications whether by Land or Water, or for the Use or Benefit of the aboriginal Inhabitants of the Country, or for Purposes of Military Defence, or as the Sites of Places of Public Worship, Schools, or other public Buildings, or as Places for the Interment of the Dead, or Places for the Recreation and Amusement of the Inhabitants of any Town or Village, or as the Sites of public Quays or Landing places on the Sea Coast or Shores of navigable Streams, or for any other Purpose of Public Safety, Convenience, Health, or Enjoyment,) there shall be paid to the said *New Zealand* Company towards the Discharge of the Principal Sum and Interest charged as aforesaid, in lieu of all and every other Claim of the said Company in respect of the said Sum, except where otherwise hereinafter provided, so long as the same or any Part thereof respectively shall remain unpaid, One Fourth Part of the Sum paid by the Purchaser in respect of every such Sale, or Alienation : Provided always it shall be lawful for the *New Zealand* Company, by any Resolution of a Majority of the Proprietors of the said Company present at any Meeting of such Proprietors, and certified under the Common Seal of such Company, to release all or any Part of the said Lands from the Monies or Payment charged thereon by the said Act or this Act, or any Part of such Monies or Payment, either absolutely or upon any Terms or Conditions, as such Proprietors may think fit.

LXXV. It shall not be lawful for the said General Assembly to repeal or interfere with all or any of the Provisions of an Act of the Session holden in the Thirteenth and Fourteenth Years of Her Majesty, Chapter Seventy, intituled *An Act empowering the* Canterbury *Association to dispose of certain Lands in* New Zealand, or of an Act passed in the Session then next following, Chapter Eighty-four, to alter and amend the said first mentioned Act; Provided always, that on the Expiration or sooner Determination of the Functions, Powers, and Authorities now vested in or lawfully exercised by the said Association, the Provisions of the present Act shall come into force as regards the Lands to which the said Acts relate.

LXXVI. It shall be lawful for the *Canterbury* Association, at any Time after a Provincial Council shall have been constituted under this Act for the Province of *Canterbury*, to transfer to the said Council all such Functions, Powers, and Authorities, and the said Council is hereby empowered to accept such Transfer upon such Terms and Conditions as shall be agreed upon between the said Council and the said Association : Provided always, that nothing contained in such Terms and Conditions shall interfere with the Rights of Her Majesty, Her Heirs and Successors, or of the *New Zealand* Company respectively ; and from and after such Time as shall be agreed upon between the said Council and the said

Association the said Council shall have and be entitled to exercise all the said Functions, Powers, and Authorities.

LXXVII. Nothing in this Act or in any Act, Law, or Ordinance to be made by the said General Assembly, or by any Provincial Assembly, shall affect or interfere with so much of An Act of the Session holden in the Fourteenth and Fifteenth Years of Her Majesty, Chapter Eighty-six, intituled, *An Act to regulate the Affairs of certain Settlements established by the* New Zealand *Company in* New Zealand, as relates to the Administration of the Fund for the public Purposes of the Settlement of *Nelson*.

LXXVIII. And whereas certain Terms of Purchase and Pasturage of Land in the Settlement of *Otago* had been issued by the *New Zealand* Company before the Fourth Day of *July* One thousand eight hundred and fifty, and the said Terms, or Part of them, were in force on that Day as Contracts between the *New Zealand* Company and the Association of Lay Members of the Free Church of *Scotland*, commonly called the *Otago* Association : And whereas by the Provisions of the said Act of the Tenth and Eleventh Years of Her Majesty, and of the said Notice given by the *New Zealand* Company, the Lands of the said Company in *New Zealand* reverted to and became vested in Her Majesty as Part of the Demesne Lands of the Crown, subject nevertheless to any Contract then subsisting in regard to any of the said Lands : And whereas it is expedient that Provision should be made to enable Her Majesty to fulfil the Contracts contained in such Terms of Purchase and Pasturage as aforesaid :

It shall be lawful for Her Majesty for that Purpose to make Provision, by way of Regulations to be contained in any Charter to be granted to the said Association, for the Disposal of the Lands to which the said Terms of Purchase and Pasturage relate, so far as the same are still in force as aforesaid, and for varying from Time to Time such Regulations, with such Consent by or on behalf of the said Association as in any such Charter or Instructions shall be specified, and for fixing the Boundaries thereof, and for enabling the said Association to transfer its Powers to the Provincial Council for the Province of *Otago* : Provided always, that no such Charter shall be granted or have Effect for any longer Term then Ten Years from the passing of this Act ; but one of Her Majesty's Principal Secretaries of State may at any Time during the Term for which such Charter shall be granted, by Writing under his Hand, extend the Term for which such Charter shall have been granted for such further Time as in his Discretion he may think fit : Provided always, that it shall not be lawful for Her Majesty, by any such Regulations as aforesaid, to diminish the Sum now payable to the *New Zealand* Company in respect of all Waste Land sold under the said Terms of Purchase, unless with the Consent of the *New Zealand* Company signified as hereinbefore provided; and during the Continuance of such Charter as aforesaid, it shall not be lawful for the said General Assembly to repeal or interfere with any such Regulations respecting Lands in *Otago*, except with such Consent by or on behalf of the *Otago* Association as in any such Charter or Instructions may be provided, and (so far as the Rights of *New Zealand* Company may be affected) with the Consent of such Company signified as hereinbefore provided ; and every Bill which shall repeal or interfere with any such Regulations shall be reserved for the Signification of Her Majesty's Pleasure thereon.

LXXIX. It shall be lawful for Her Majesty, by any such Letters Patent as aforesaid, or Instructions under Her Majesty's Signet and Sign Manual, or signified through One of Her Majesty's Principal Secretaries of State, to delegate to the Governor any of the Powers hereinbefore reserved to Her Majesty respecting the Removal of Superintendents of Provinces and the Regulation of the Sale, Letting, Disposal, and Occupation of Waste Lands, the Establishment of Municipal Corporations, and the Preservation of aboriginal Laws, Customs, and Usages. .

LXXX. In the Construction of this Act the Term " Governor" shall mean the Person for the Time being lawfully administering the Government of *New Zealand;* and for the Purposes of this Act *"New Zealand"* shall be held to include all Territories, Islands, and Countries lying between Thirty-three Degrees of South Latitude and Fifty Degrees of South Latitude, and One hundred and sixty-two Degrees of East Longitude and One hundred and seventy-three Degrees of West Longitude, .reckoning from the Meridian of *Greenwich.*

LXXXI. This Act shall be proclaimed in *New Zealand* by the Governor thereof within Six Weeks after a Copy of such Act shall have been received by such Governor, and, save as herein expressly provided, shall take effect in *New Zealand* from the Day of such Proclamation thereof.

LXXXII. The Proclamation of this Act, and all Proclamations to be made under the Provision thereof, shall be published in the *New Zealand* Government Gazette.

SCHEDULE referred to in the foregoing Act. .

Governor,	£2,500
Chief Justice,	1,000
Puisne Judge,	800
Establishment of the General Government,	4,700
Native Purposes,	7,000
	£16,000

WORKS ON CONFEDERATION.

FOR SALE BY

DAWSON BROTHERS, MONTREAL.

The Constitutions of the United States,—Containing the Declaration of Independence, the Articles of Confederation, the Constitution adopted, and the Constitutions of the Several States. $1.50

Story, Joseph. LL.D.—Commentaries on the Constitutions of the United States.—2 Vols. 8vo. $6.00
> Do.   do. abridged. 8vo. $2.75.
> Do.   do.   do.   12mo. $1.00.

Marshall, Chief Justice.—Writings upon the Federal Constitution.—8vo. $2.25.

Rawle, Wm., LL.D.—View of the Constitution of the United States.—8vo. $4.00.

Sergeant, Thos.—Constitutional Law, being a View of the Constitutional Points decided in the Courts of the United States.—8vo. $3.00.

McKinney, M.—Explanatory statement of the Government of the United States. $1.00.

Curtis, Geo. J.—History of the Constitution of the United States.—2 Vols., 8vo. $4.00.

Duer, President. Lectures on the Constitutional Jurisprudence of the United States.—1 Vol., small 8vo. $1.50.

Cocke, William R.—Constitutional History of the United States.—Vol. 1 only published, 8vo. $1.75.

Baldwin, Judge.—Origin and Nature of the Constitution and Government of the United States.—8vo. $1.50.

The Federalist.—8vo. $2.50.

Chipman, N., LL.D.—Principles of Government.—8vo. $2.50.

Lieber, Francis, LL.D.—On Civil Liberty and Self-Government.—8vo. $2.25.

Goodrich, Chas. D.—Lowell Lectures on the Science of Government.—8vo. $1.00.

Trescott, W. H.—Diplomatic History of the Administrations of Washington and Adams, 1789-1801.—12mo. $1.00.

Elliot, Jonathan.—Debates in the Several State Conventions, on the Adoption of the Federal Constitution of 1787, with the Journal of the Federal Convention, the Virginia and Kentucky Conventions, and other important documents.—5 Vols., 8vo. $15.00.

The Works of Thomas Jefferson.—9 Vols., 8vo. $15.00.

Hall, Benj.—Official Opinions of the Attorneys-General of the United States, advising the Presidents, and Heads of Departments, and Expounding the Constitution and Public Laws.—8 Vols., 8vo. $20.00.

The Proceedings and Debates of the Convention of Pennsylvania to propose amendments to the Constitution in 1837.—14 Vols., 8vo. $14.00.

Journal of the Constitutional Convention of Massachusetts in 1853.—8vo. $3.50.

Official Report of the Debates and Proceedings in the State Convention of Massachussetts of 1853.—3 Vols, 8vo. $6.00.

Journal of the Convention for framing a Constitution of Government for the State of Massachusetts Bay, held in 1779-80, with illustrative documents.—8vo. $2.50.

The Proceedings of the Conventions of 1776 and 1790, and the minutes of the Convention which formed the Constitution of Pennsylvania.—8vo. $2.00.

Gibbes, R. W.—Documentary History of South Carolina.—3 Vols., 8vo. $4.50.

Calhoun, John C.—Disquisition on Government, and on the Government of the United States.—8vo. $2.75.

Debates in the Convention of California on the formation of the State Constitution in 1849. $1.50.

COLONIAL.

Cartwright, R. J., M.P.P.—Remarks on the Militia of Canada. 20 cents.

Letters by a Backwoodsman. 25 cents.

Thompson.—The Future Government of Canada. 15 cents.

The Northern Kingdom, by a Colonist. 12½ cents.

The Proposed Federal Constitution. 5 cents.

Speech on the Proposed Union of the B. N. A. Provinces, by the Hon. A. T. Galt. 10 cents.

Hamilton, P. S., of Nova Scotia.—The Union of the Colonies. 25 cents.

Cavendish, Sir H.—Debates in the House of Commons in 1774, on the Bill to Provide for the Government of the Province of Quebec. $2.25.

Mackintosh, Sir James, Speech on the Civil Government of Canada, contained in his works.—1 Vol., 8vo. $2.00.

Chalmers, Geo.—Opinions of Eminent Lawyers on Colonial Matters. $8.00.

ON THE BRITISH CONSTITUTION.

DeLolme.—Constitution of England, by Macgregor. $1.00.

Brougham, Lord.—The British Constitution. $1.25.

Creasy, Sir E.—Rise and Progress of the British Constitution. $1.00.

Mill, John Stuart.—On Representative Government. $1.00.

Hallam, H.—Constitutional History of England. $3.75.

May, Thos. E.   Do.   do. $2.50.

Bennett, Thos. R.—Popular Manual of the Constitutional History of England. 62 cents.

CPSIA information can be obtained
at www.ICGtesting.com
Printed in the USA
BVHW040159141118
533011BV00009B/129/P